TUNISIA

A Journey Through a Country that Works

TUNISIA

A Journey Through a Country that Works

Georgie Anne Geyer

STACEY INTERNATIONAL

TUNISIA
A Journey Through a Country that Works

© Georgie Anne Geyer 2003

STACEY INTERNATIONAL
128 Kensington Church Street
London W8 4BH
Tel: +44 (0)207 221 7166; fax: +44 (0)207 792 9288
E-mail: enquiries@stacey-international.co.uk
Website: www.stacey-international.co.uk

ISBN: 1 900988 437

CIP Data:
A catalogue record for this book is available from the British Library

Printed and bound in the UK by Biddles Ltd.

*To my dear friend Lynne, whose spirit
will always be with us.*

Acknowledgements

I am pleased to acknowledge the help I have received from innumerable people in preparing this book on an exceptional and instructive country. My visits to Tunisia were, of course, my first inspiration. During those visits in 1972, 1997, 1998, twice in 1999 and then again in 2002, I spoke with dozens of Tunisians on all levels – my thanks to all of them for their frank expressions of their hopes and fears. My years of experience as a correspondent in the Middle East from 1969 onwards stood me in good stead as I was able to back these interviews up with experiences across the Arab world. Many talks with American and other foreign diplomats, businessmen and thinkers were invaluable.

My interviews within the government were particularly facilitated by the official spokesman of the President, Abdewahab Abdallah, who has my deepest thanks for his efficient arrangements for my interviews with President Zine El Abidine Ben Ali. I am equally indebted to Oussama Romdhani and his expert Tunisian External Communications Agency, with particular thanks going to his assistant Bochra Malki. Two Tunisian ambassadors to Washington during the 1990s, in particular, Ambassador Noureddine Mejdoub and Ambassador Hatem Atallah, provided invaluable assistance in understanding and analysing their country, as especially did Minister of Foreign Affairs Habib ben Yahia and Minister of Culture Abdelbaki Hermassi, whose insights into their country's development were invaluable.

Since I am a working journalist with a thrice-weekly international affairs column, the added financial and other responsibilities of taking time to prepare a book were considerably eased by a small, but most welcome, research and travel grant from the Tunisian American Chamber of Commerce. They have my thanks. I also want to thank my congenial and endlessly curious friends and companions who so graciously and joyfully shared the June 1999 tourist trip to the country: Ambassador Robert Oakley, State Department diplomat Phyllis Oakley, *Washington Post* diplomatic correspondent Don Oberdorfer, his wife Laura Oberdorfer and businesspeople Stanton and Dickie Dossett. It was on part of that trip that we discovered the 'road-with-the-white-line-down-the-centre', and their insights were important in testing and/or confirming my earlier ones.

In London, my thanks surely go to Stacey International, an unusual company which has prepared and published unusually beautiful books on the Middle East, capturing the historic and spiritual essence of the peoples and the countries at a time when virtually the only coverage of the area was of violence and chaos. In particular, I want to thank Tom Stacey, Max Scott, Caroline Singer and Graham Edwards for their professional and creative approach and work.

For checking on the history of a complicated country, I relied on two accomplished historians, Nejib Ben Lazreg, an archaeologist who works with the Bardo Museum in Tunis. He read and corrected the entire manuscript, as did my respected old friend, Professor Edmund Ghareeb, professor of Middle Eastern Studies at the American University in Washington DC. To both, I owe a special debt of gratitude, for such careful and meticulous work on someone else's manuscript can be as taxing as the writing itself. For every other possible kind of work, from Internet research, to uncovering and locating dozens of not-easily-found old books on Tunisia to the day-to-day work on the book, I can never give sufficient thanks to my indomitable assistant, Rita Tiwari. Her enthusiasm, her intelligent observations and her good judgement were invaluable.

The responsibility for the book is, of course, totally mine, but I hope that the abovementioned will feel that the book belongs to all of them.

Georgie Anne Geyer
Washington DC
August 2003

Contents

1. The South: *Preparing for the Tour de France*

*'Either you're born into democracy or you have to make it
happen, and if you have to make it happen, you have to go
step by step – and you only have so many years to do it.'*

**Tunisian sociologist and Minister of Culture,
Dr. Abdelbaki Hermassi**

The Road Taken

The desert glittered that morning like a field of diamonds in the
morning sun. Beams of light danced off the grains of sand and
catapulted across the dunes. There was nothing on the horizon at all.
An unbroken line separated the azure blue sky from the barren desert
and seemed to stretch all about us in a perfect, protective circle. It was
a world without shadows and seemingly without a living soul. Not a
house, not a dwelling, neither a cave nor a caravan, nowhere a tree or
a cactus, and, except for the road, no trace at all of the hand of man.

But there was the road, and it seemed to be actually going
somewhere. It was a good, clear road, simple and thin and black,
neither immodest in its pretentions nor overbearing in its aspect. It
looked like an arrow that was pointing across the desert – but, to
where?

Our small group – myself, five friends from Washington and a driver – were driving in a small, patient car through the long-forsaken south of Tunisia. This is where the vast and forbidding Sahara begins, where raging storms can propel desert sands as far as the southernmost coasts of France, Spain and Turkey. We were somewhere between the southern city of Tozeur in the south-west of the country, with its strange, stark sand lakes, its oases as lush as little African Gardens of Eden and its sweeping plateaus of eroded hills – and the languid, sensuous Isle of Djerba off the south-eastern coast. For centuries, the original inhabitants of the south, the mysterious Berber people, resignedly called this region 'the country of hardships'. Historically, Tunisian governments used the threat of this end-of-the-line place, as powerful men have often used the desert, as a place of exile and of punishment. Even the founder of the modern Tunisian state, Habib Bourguiba, was once imprisoned there by the French, stranded for many months on the edge of the Sahara.

But it was also a strangely beautiful land. People meant it when they said 'you can hear the silence', a perception that is not only poetic, but scientifically true, since sand absorbs the noises of men.

As for us, we had been lulled into a sleepy mood that day by the rhythm of the car, the extravagant sun and vivid colours and by the occasional mirage that appeared like a watery blue spectre floating somewhere out there on the horizon. Sometimes these mirages would come complete with date trees, sometimes without; always they would arise suddenly, to taunt and tempt us and then wickedly disappear. It was a dreamy day until, suddenly, we saw *it*. Quite a way ahead of us on this neat, black, orderly little road, coming out of nowhere, we saw something that appeared to be standing right in the middle of our well-built, solid, jet-black road striking eastward towards the sea.

At first, the vision was hazy: could this be another mirage? Then, very slowly, the image came into view. We hooded our eyes with our hands to try and focus on what seemed to be a lone figure and then we squinted to make out what, or who, it could be. In most of the world's deserts, you will find faith-crazed mystics, money-crazed oil-tappers and amateur explorers like us, but somehow this vision didn't seem to fit any of those categories.

'Oh no, there's nothing there,' one of the men said. 'We're imagining it.'

'No, no, no, it's more than that,' the driver interjected.

Indeed, as we came closer to the image, two figures began to take form. Finally we could see that our apparition was, in truth, made up of two ordinary Tunisian workmen, small, wiry chaps who seemed totally dedicated to their work out in that blazing hot desert sun. With their jeep right there on the road with them, and a small bright red warning flag waving smartly in the light spring breeze from atop a swaying pole, the two workmen were as busy and as focused as if they were constructing a skyscraper in Manhattan. First one would stoop over and do something on the road; then the other would move the small jeep to keep up with his friend. Their movements were slow, but deliberate, rather like a workingman's ballet. So far as we could see, they spoke not at all.

Finally, as we came closer, we understood what their act really was. They were painting a white line down this isolated desert road!

As we passed them, the two men waved in a proud and friendly manner and then simply went on with their work. Behind us, the road had a smart white line right down the middle, but ahead of us there stretched only the straight, spartan black highway, its day clearly coming. Our group was silent for a while, for we realised that we had seen something so simple and so clear that it was, in its way and in today's world, remarkable. On an everyday level, these two workmen were merely doing their assigned job. But in the greater and more imaginative scheme of things, out on that vast desert they were preparing for the future of their country, challenging and pre-empting destiny and readying themselves and their nation for a unique future that, even ten years before, no-one could have imagined. Their seemingly small piece of work was actually one of the tens of thousands of movements leading towards the development of a region that had long been consigned to the peripheries of mankind.

Despite the fact that, on that trip in the spring of 1999, our group had met with leading officials, diplomats, journalists, artists and thinkers, we all came to think of those two workmen, making their bold and confident line across the sand, as the leitmotif of the country today. To us, they would always personify what the

Tunisians like to call their 'Epoch of Development', their 'Great Change' or their 'Small Enlightenment'. Later, in Tunis, I mentioned 'the road' to a university professor and he nodded, pleased. He understood well what it was all about.

'It's because the Tour de France will come there soon,' he answered sagely, with a pleased nod of his head.

What Manner of Country?

Despite its generally non-violent fight for independence from France, which left it an independent nation in 1956, and despite its enviable record for rational reform in the 1960s and '70s, Tunisia would have given anyone who paused to look at it in the sobering 1980s little cause for hope. How could that beautiful but vulnerably placed country on the north coast of Africa ever really 'make it'? It was a small country, its land base a mere 63,170 square miles, which made it close to the size of the American states of Missouri or Washington or to the south-east Asian country of Cambodia. Historically and archaeologically, its riches were beyond comparison. Many historians said that Tunisia had more valuable heritage sites for its size than almost any other country in the world; riches that had emerged in the dawn of history from virtually every one of the great cultures and empires of the Mediterranean.

Tunisia's nine million people represented a handsome blend of all of these cultures. They are small-boned men and women of light olive complexion, and an average height of five foot seven inches. Most have brown eyes and short black hair. The Tunisian women are often astonishingly beautiful, with dark hair and almond eyes, yet there were also often blue eyes to be found in the mix, as if to say, as so many conquerers had done, 'I was there too!' Outside the more remote villages, most Tunisians wear western dress, although for relaxation they will wear the loose and graceful *burnous* robe. But the men usually top even their western suits with the beloved Tunisian *chechia*, the little red brimless cap worn by most Tunisian men. The *chechia* industry is typical of Tunisian initiative. Local craftsmen designed and developed it and domestic businessmen now sell it avidly across the Mediterranean. Although they are an Arab people, with a large mixture of French and Italian blood from the

19th and 20th centuries, the Tunisians have always been convinced in their hearts that they are a different people as, indeed, they are.

The first impression the visitor has is that the sweet, enticing, lyrical beauty of the country is a Mediterranean dream painted in blue and white, from the glowing azure blue of the sea to the neat white villas that seem to tumble down to the eastern seacoast like petals dropping into the sea. The extravagant beauty of the coast stretches like a necklace of little cities from the capital Tunis, around the thumb of Cap Bon, only 85 sea miles from Sicily, and then southward along the coast to the place where Tunisia eventually meets the Sahara and black Africa. Sousse, Hammamet, Monastir… these are indolent towns, cities historically admired for their luxury (and sometimes, their sheer wickedness). From the baths of Roman times to the elaborate receptions of the ruling dynastic Turkish-related Beys in the 19th century to the joys of the millions of tourists who now flock there every year, everywhere one experiences beauty and the bounty of sensuous impressions.

The other Arabs like to say that the Tunisians have 'light blood'; what the French call *la douceur arabe*. For although they are a deeply serious people, there is also a charmingly romantic side to their character, a pleasing sentiment which matches their landscape. This Tunisia is a world filled with the beguiling scent of orange trees, lemon flowers and jasmine and at times imbued with a kind of dazed tranquility. When the artist Paul Klee rode down the coast from Tunis on a slow train in 1914, he wrote in his diary: 'Fabulous, right on the sea, jagged and rectangular, then jagged again… I try to paint. The reeds and bushes provide a beautiful patchwork rhythm…' Klee would have been delighted to see the extent to which his coast has today become a cultural centre for the entire Mediterranean region.

Tunisia is in fact composed of a number of areas, and part of the fascination of the country is that, within such a small physical area, these regions are all so different. The northern region, the mountainous 'Tell,' with its high peaks reaching to 5,000 feet, has the richest soil and the largest population of all. The central part of the country, the 'Steppe,' is made up of barren lands with bad soil and low rainfall and leads into the 'South' or the Sahara. Then there is the coastal region or the 'Sahel', the region that gave birth to and formed independent Tunisia's first president, the redoubtable Habib Bourguiba, as well as to an inordinate number of its leaders and businessmen. For the Sahel had not only fertile land, but was also known historically for its commercial ties with the outside world, which since ancient times has given its people a sense of confident openness to the world. The Sahel also had more family solidarity than tribal solidarity, with all that meant in terms of the traditions of self-help. Some historians have said that the dominant culture of olive cultivation, in which ten to fifteen years must pass before the first crop appears, has served to instill in the Sahelians a capacity for delayed gratification, and that could well be true.

At times, there is an almost historical zaniness about the country: its place-names, for example, are of so many different origins – Arabic, Berber, Latin and Punic – that they were first written in Arabic script, then translated into French by the French colonisers. It was those early Frenchmen of the euphemistically-named 'Protectorate' who drew up the first maps and gazeteers and who committed what one writer has called the 'linguistic atrocity' of adopting not the correct form of the place-names, but that used locally by the inhabitants, or even a form that the French could pronounce more easily. 'The result is like a map of London with the place-names transcribed into Cockney,' the British writer and diplomat Michael Tomkinson wrote in *Michael Tomkinson's Tunisia*, his evocative prose-and-photograph book on the country. Thus, 'Ben' is the North African version of the true Arabic *ibn* or 'son of'. 'Bou' is the Tunisian version of the Arabic *abu* or 'father of' and *funduq*, the Arabic for 'hotel' came to be spelt as 'fondouk' in Tunisia, where they were really the quarters in the medina allotted to early European merchants and envoys by the early Hafsid rulers.

Yet, while Tunisia is rich in inhabitants, as well as in lore and legend, and while Tunisians are trained in agriculture and in some small industry, the country nevertheless sits geographically in a troubled neighbourhood. It is a small country, jammed between Muammar Khadafy's Libya, and Algeria with its savage Islamic fundamentalist civil wars that had killed upwards of 200,000 by the late 1990s. Tunisia has no great natural resources, nor even any oil, and its leaders were 'foolish' enough to boast about that. They had eschewed Arab nationalism early on, preferring instead a gradual, organic development, something that surely sets them apart from the whole region. Finally, it is a country of mixed ethnic groups – Arab, Berber, African, French, Jewish, Turkish, Moorish – and it came close, during the troubled 1980s, to joining much of the rest of the world in serious religious conflict. In fact, it became the first Arab country to be seriously threatened with Islamic fundamentalism, and it was considered to be so close to total internal breakdown in the late 1980s, that the French newspaper *Le Monde* often editorialised on the interesting question of: 'When is Tunisia going to collapse?'

All across the Arab world, nations seemed to have tried everything: post-colonial authoritarian dictatorships, military rule, Arab nationalist Nasserite regimes, Ba'athist secular governments, tribally-rooted monarchies, the Muslim Brotherhood, Islamic fascism and Muslim puritanism… but none brought either prosperity or justice to the people. The Arab world had the lowest percentage of foreign investment of any region in the world, about four percent by the turn of the 20th century; hundreds of thousands of boys were emerging from universities with only rote learning of the Koran and no skills they could use in the modern world, and by the turn of the century, Islamic terrorism was growing everywhere, threatening Arab regimes and the West alike. Across western Europe and the United States, and even within certain countries of the Arab world, analysts and scholars proclaimed that 'nothing had worked' in the Arab world, that there were no models and that, even worse, there were no principles, no formulas and apparently no experiences on which to draw.

These questions of politics, economics and social welfare – which were essentially questions of governance – had been conflicting with one another across the Muslim world throughout the 20th century. But they really came to a head with the terrorist threats against America on September 11th, 2001 and the subsequent American invasion of Afghanistan and then Iraq. Suddenly the entire world sat up and took notice. 'Something had to be done' to modernise the Arab world but commentators repeated, as always, how sad and unfortunate it was that there were no models.

But this was not true even then. There *was* a formula and there *was* a model, based upon the principles that the Tunisians had employed and upon the experiences that they had carefully crafted for themselves. A liberalised Islam? Tunisia had achieved this in the mid-19th century. An economic model that was providing more for its people every year, while easing them carefully into the modern world? Tunisia was already doing that. A country where women were free and productive? This was such an old story in Tunisia that the question about women's liberation evoked only yawns. Political development? It was underway, albeit more slowly than progress in the other areas.

The example was there all along, and still is. The question should have been: 'Why had nobody noticed?' Or as we might paraphrase it: 'Why had most of the rest of the world not only chosen to ignore, but had even at times chosen to revile and disdain the Tunisian experience?' But that comes later.

Discovering Tunisia

When I first travelled to Tunisia in 1992 for my journalistic work, I found an historically charming and potentially abundant country which had, however, retained a veneer of 'Third Worldism' and was still nursing a hangover from the fundamentalist threat, which had only that very year begun to abate. When I went back in 1997, the country was thriving and I had many fascinating discussions about philosophy and development. It was then that I discovered the beguiling South. In 1998, I had my first interview with the Tunisian President Zine El Abidine Ben Ali in Carthage Palace, and I was fascinated with the efficient and productive manner in which the encounter was arranged and carried through. When I returned in the spring of 1999 with friends, the country was deeply involved in the economic changes it had to make to join the European Union. In October of 1999, I had my second interview with President Ben Ali. I returned once more in March of 2002 and was able to penetrate far more deeply into the historic Islamic and Tunisian cultures and to discover why Islam had reformed so early and so productively here, while so much of the rest of the Middle East was still stagnating and struggling.

This, then, is the story of those trips and of my research, together with 30 years of intensive journalistic coverage of the entire Middle East. This does not purport to be an authoritative history, although it draws deeply on history. Rather, it is an attempt to understand how and why this country has chosen to develop so wisely, when so few others have been able to do so. This book is not so much a work of straightforward travel literature, but is more perhaps a new kind of 'political travel literature' or even 'developmental political literature'.

I began with the examples of what I could actually see, then looked at how the government, the private sector and the Tunisian people were manning specific projects, and finally I considered the ideas and principles behind those projects.

During my first trip to Tunisia in 1992, I wrote that while Tunisia, like every development experiment, was imperfect, it was a 'country that worked'. When I returned in 1997, I was leafing through one of their investment magazines, which was trying to lure foreign investors to the country. On every single page was a square in the upper corner, with bold letters pronouncing: 'Tunisia: The Country That Works!'

So What About the Tour de France?
The world-famous race may not have arrived in Tunisia yet, but many other foreigners and foreign projects were coming, even in that forgotten and long-desperate South or 'Sud,' as Tunisians like to call it.

Not far from Tozeur, our guide took us on a very bumpy trip through the terrestrial skyscape where the newest *Star Wars* film had been shot. For more than an hour, we bounced up and down a moonscape of dry, barren mountains, our van seeming to slip and slide across the low valleys. Who could have imagined that such a strange wasteland could have been used for anything? The Tunisians were of course immensely pleased with the wonderful critiques their eerily frightening landscapes were receiving around the world.

'Why had the film-makers chosen Tunisia?' I asked our guide at one point.

'That's easy,' the Tunis official answered, with a self-confidence rare for this part of the world. 'We have been preparing for years, building the roads and the airports down here and we have good hotels for the crews. We created the opportunity, and when the opportunity came, we were ready.'

All across the South, ancient Berber villages were dug into the sides of the mountains. Fortresses clung to the sides of the cliffs, villages were built so defensively as to repel the conquering hordes. Then we found still another example of the 'Tunisian way' in the villages and houses of the historic Berber people, who, as the original tribal people of this part of Africa, had long been the most backward in the country. Yet just outside another town, Douz, we visited a modern Berber village which showed how they are being integrated and amalgamated into the predominantly Arabised, Europeanised society of the North. In the early 1990s, at their request, the Berber tribespeople here had been brought down from their poor and ancient fortified hillside town and settled into new houses. The new town was unusually pleasant, with neat white houses built in the arched Tunisian style, small green yards, an infirmary and, of course, the school.

But what was so important – and what was typical of the Tunisian model and method of modernisation – was the fact that the government's social planners had left the ruins of the ancient village right there, next to the new town. In their new homes, they could see, feel, touch, smell and visit their old ones. Today, the villages are out in the open, for they are now protected by the larger polity, to which they now belong. Not only have they not been left behind in the modernisation process, but they have also neither been uprooted nor sundered from their past, as has happened with such sobering consequences in so many other countries. Sometimes in Tunisia, where they are still struggling to come up with honestly descriptive terms for what they are doing, they call it 'modernity with authenticity'.

That same day, the guide took us to the ancient village of Matmata to see the Berbers' other homes, their excavated underground cave-houses. Obviously a people with a special talent for odd housing schemes, the Berbers built strange 'skyscraper' complexes, remarkable for their time, and often five storeys tall. Known as *ghorfas* (these were probably fortified granaries), they had no windows and the builders pressed the images of hands and feet on the ceilings to protect them from the evil spirits outside. This same curious people then turned downwards and dug enormous holes more than 20 feet deep into the desert ground and scooped out rooms to live. Actually, the Berbers had a trinity of odd houses: cave dwellings, pit dwellings and cliff dwellings.

More is known about the Berbers' housing, which of course one can actually see, than is known about them as a people. There is no written Berber language, and the term 'Berber', which came from the fussy Greek 'barberio' or 'barbarian', only indicates certain well-defined linguistic and social characteristics. It appears that they are Caucasians, and many still have light-coloured eyes today, although historians claim that, sometime in their 300,000-year history, they had two roots, one in Yemen and the other in sub-Saharan Africa. The Greek historian Herodotus described them, in words that again reflect the romantic propensity of so many parts of Tunisia, as 'people who never dream' and 'the only people in the world to do without names'. One of the Berber tribes, he added, giving spice to their reputation, had womenfolk who 'wear leather bands round their ankles, one for each of their lovers.' So far as we know, there are no records of how many of these bands the women might have worn at any one time.

As Tunisia's rich and varied – but often enough, violent – history unfolded, the Berber world was overrun by Carthaginians, Romans, Vandals, Byzantines, Arabs, Normans, Sicilians, Andalusians, Turks, French and many more peoples. In fact, the eternally assaulted but apparently infinitely adaptable Berbers changed religion no fewer than 12 times during their historic ordeals, finally settling, with their accustomed practical good sense, on Islam which they, like the vast majority of Tunisians, hold as their national religion today. But things are very different today: in Matmata, we discovered that one of the underground cave dwellings was used for the homestead of the *Star Wars* movie's Luke Skywalker character.

Then, on another section of the east-west road across the southern desert, where there had seemed to be nothing but horizon, we suddenly spotted a small wooden building. It turned out to be a prime example of the personal enterprise shown by Tunisians, evidence of yet another of Tunisia's policies to encourage private and individual initiative.

From a distance, it appeared to be a kind of jerry-built shack, centred around a small desert garden. But as we came closer, we realised that this was actually a very charming, cosmopolitan-type café, with touches of French style in the essentially Arabic and North African fashion. It seemed to be sitting there all alone and, although certainly modest, looked rather proud of itself. Although it was nothing more than an assemblage of woven fences and a simple, half-open bar, the café had something oddly stylish about it, with an array of business cards and drawings of people from all over the world glued to the walls. Outside, there was an attractive small garden, and a large, brightly-painted Tunisian vase announcing boldly 'Tarzan's Café'. This was clearly a place you could not possibly pass by.

Tarzan himself turned out to be a tall, lean, good-looking man with a gleaming smile. Tarzan Belgacem was his full name, he said. This Tunisian 'Rick' in what seemed like a re-telling of the movie *Casablanca,* fixed us Turkish coffee and told his story. 'I came here in 1985,' he said. 'I worked in hotels in Douz and got tired of it all, so I came out here when the government built the road. Rich people from Tunis come out now and beg me to let them stay overnight. I say, "No, I have no space." About 400 people come by in the summer season.' Then he smiled and added proudly that, 'the drivers who come by call me the "Lion of the Desert".'

Perhaps our meeting with this modern-day 'king of the desert' could be dismissed as our updated version of Omar al-Mukhtar, an early hero of the Libyan desert wars against the foreigners – an 'accident of voyaging', as the romantic writer Antoine de Saint-Exupéry once called such pleasant and unexpected meetings – were it not for the fact that, in Tunisia, this kind of small business has blossomed in the last 20 years. Today there are commercial brothers and sisters of Tarzan's Café everywhere in Tunisia. Later, when I wrote a short column featuring him and sent him a copy, he read it out on Tunisian TV. Such are the roars of these new-style, free enterprise, Tunisian desert lions.

Next I was to discover yet another secret of the Tunisian way: tolerance and respect for the other. These were qualities that were regarded as not only noble and right, but – typical for the Tunisians – also good for development.

Off the southern coasts, one comes to the islands. Some observers even today cling to the theory that the smaller island of Kerkennah and the larger islands of Djerba, which push out into the Mediterranean just northwest of Libya in the Bay of Gabes, were once the 'lost continent of Atlantis', supposedly destroyed in a great tidal wave. This is important not for its accuracy, but because it reflects the sweetly, delusional quality of the air, sun and sea that hangs over so many places in Tunisia.

The story that truly defines Djerba, however, is another that is repeated over and over again when the sultry breezes blow off the Mediterranean. It seems that when Ulysses landed on the magical island in ancient times, a strange madness overtook his entire group. Once they had eaten the local lotus blossom – one bite would suffice, so they said – they refused to go home, completely forgot their families and countries, and dreamed of remaining forever in that beautiful place. Finally, Ulysses had to bring them back to the boat by force and hold them down with chains from their obsession.

In Tunisia, it is just best not to question the 'fact' that Ulysses landed there on his voyage home from Troy in Homer's *Odyssey*, for Tunisians do so like the story. I would not myself dare to challenge such a defining tale because somehow it has, as well, the feel of sensuous truth about it. One day, when we crossed by ferry from the mainland to Djerba, the breezes were blowing in such a delicious and intoxicating manner, and the sky was so extravagantly blue and compelling, that I had to rouse my own greatest will to leave. Sadly, I did not find any lotus blossoms, but I did find Tunisia's unique Jewish colony and memories so ancient, so filled with a sense of overcoming tragedy and destiny, that their story makes even practical people shiver with respect.

Djerba holds what is reputed to be the earliest surviving Jewish settlement in the world. Its few thousand remaining members believe that their famous synagogue, which is exquisitely designed and obviously ancient, was built 2,500 years ago. This suggests that pockets of Jewish people came here after the Babylonians' destruction of the First Temple of Jerusalem in the 6th century BC. The famous Djerba synagogue, 'the Ghriba', is a spacious, delicate wooden building. Inside is a handsome melange of Tunisian blues and whites, mottled greens, weathered wooden seats and ancient Torahs decorated with silver. It is a fabled place; the faithful say that a stone from the original temple was carried here, and during their services, they still speak of King Nebuchadnezzar II, against whom the Jews revolted after 17 years of Babylon's yoke. The synagogue's gold and silver ornaments were a target of the Nazi armies under General Erwin Rommel, who criss-crossed Tunisia during World War Two, his troops singing the evocative German ballad *Lili Marlene*.

It was this original voyage, in the 6th century BC, that marked the beginning of the Jewish people's 'Diaspora' and, unlike synagogues elsewhere in the world, the liturgy in the Ghriba has not changed to this day. What has changed, however, is the fact that Israeli visitors receive temporary passports when they come on pilgrimage and that the government's policy officially encourages Tunisian Jews to resume their ancient links with this open and tolerant country. In fact, Foreign Minister Habib Ben Yahia has often called for a 'reconciliation of the sons of Abraham'.

We stopped in the busy Djerba souk afterwards, and I found Youssif Gamoun, a handsome master jeweller from Djerba's Jewish community. He was in his gorgeous silver shop, where he hammers exquisite designs on everything from holy pieces for synagogues abroad to lovely personal jewellery. He related to me the history that his family had passed on to him. 'We believe we came after the destruction of the Temple,' he said. 'A group of Jews came with a stone from the Temple and built this synagogue around it. That stone is now part of the wall.'

I thought afterwards that only in Tunisia could one find this picture of 3,000 Jews in an Arab country: respected citizens, prospering with their silver shops, their yeshiva schools and a young community which, by all accounts, enjoyed the best of relations with their Muslim neighbours and the small number of Christians.

Still more amazing was the fact that, if you drove northwards just a couple of hours from Djerba and from the heart of the Berber territory, you would come to the great walled Islamic city of Kairouan, founded in 660 AD by the Prophet Mohammed's followers a few years after his death. Kairouan was important: it was the 'Mecca' from which the Muslims Islamicised Africa. It is said that when Kairouan was founded by a group of Muslims who journeyed from Arabia, the plain around the marshy, scrubby site they chose was full of snakes and savage wild animals such as lions, hyenas and cheetahs. But the Muslim leader, a man named Okba, spoke to the wild beasts: 'Go away and may God have mercy on you.' And soon all the beasts were seen leading their young away from the sacred city.

One finds unusual memories and monuments everywhere in Tunisia. You can kick up a stone in many places and stumble upon a Roman mosaic, or dig and find an ancient cellar where the early Tunisian Christians hid from the Romans during the conquest. And yet there are ancient public baths with modern solar panels, and special hotels which treat you with hot mineral mud and sea water.

Particularly in the northwest, you can easily come across villages that are even more starkly white than the coastal cities. In towns like Testour, many people still speak Spanish because they are direct descendants of the Moors who fled here between the 15th and 17th centuries. In some elegant homes, you will see pictures of the Turkish reformer, Kemal Atatürk, whose reformist ideas found such a meeting of minds here that the founder of modern Tunisia, Habib Bourguiba, was often called the 'Arab Atatürk.' There is also a tradition of ancient queens in Tunisia which mirrors the advanced role of women in the country today. The most prominent was the woman they called 'El-Kahina', 'The Priestess' or 'The Prophetess'. She led the final Berber resistance against the Arabs and may well have been of the Jewish faith; legend has it that she was 127 years old when she finally died, defeated in battle but still so beautiful that her conqueror, an Arab general, cut off her head and sent it in a bag to the Caliph to prove that he had triumphed over a woman, and not a magician. The men of the era, jealous and humbled by this woman, were only able to rise above the humiliation of acknowledging her courage and genius by denying she was a military leader, and casting her as a shaman.

What characterises Tunisia more than any other country in the region is its movement. Here is a people who, like our road in the South, are going somewhere. In other parts of the Middle East and North Africa, many people waste their lives away, waiting on park benches, sitting hunched in doorways, preening themselves for changes that are yet to come, and probably never will. And so their pride turns to political and social rage and their waiting ends in violence.

But in Tunisia, people act purposefully, because they have a lot to do: they have good jobs, they own their own homes, there is education for everyone, social insurance, a representative government, a responsible leadership, a practical set of principles behind the state, a poverty that is diminishing every day, planned economic moves and virtually unlimited hope for the future. Today, even in 'the country of hardships' in the South, urban life is prospering. The blue and white cities proudly display their Moorish, Islamic and French influences, with their picturesque artistic tiles, latticework and, everywhere, flowers and the scent of orange blossom. Never would one see a child – a boy or girl – without a school uniform and a packet of books on his or her back. Every town has a family planning clinic, which is announced in large and prominent black letters, which the majority of women attend without the slightest embarrassment.

Almost unbelievable, in terms of its past, the South has now become a major tourist destination. Travellers come to enjoy the special rates in its charming new hotels, its large swimming pools and trips on the beautifully polished old train, the Lezard Rouge, built by a wealthy early 19th century phosphate miner, which takes you on a spellbinding ride through dramatic canyons that rival many in the American south-west.

Finally, we discovered that a group of dedicated scientists are now working in Medenine on one of the furthest reaches of the Sahara, their watchword being 'Stop the Sahara!' The fact that 75 researchers and scientists from the country's Institute of Arid Regions, plus 102,000 men and women – 4.4 percent of the country's working population in other institutes – are endeavouring to halt the advancement of the desert, shows the degree to which Tunisia is using the most rational scientific methods of the modern age to control the vagaries of the beguiling, treacherous Sahara. In fact, Tunisia was the first Arab country to create a Ministry of the Environment, and law requires that every city and town have an 'Avenue of the Environment'.

Western diplomats in Tunis call the new infrastructure and development in the long-forgotten South extraordinary. 'We have unlocked the landlocked regions, especially in the South,' the

Tunisian Foreign Minister Habib Ben Yahia told me on my first trip to the region. 'That's the tissue of society and it's not so obvious to a visitor, but it's how you should really judge a society.'

I decided to move on, from the projects and the examples to the ideas and principles behind them. My first two stops would be with two of the most accomplished and admired men in Tunisia.

Democracy is Not Instant Coffee

I found Foreign Minister Habib Ben Yahia, one of Tunisia's most experienced and respected diplomats, in his office in the exquisite Dar el Bey just on the edge of Tunis' lovely Medina or old city. This 17th century palace was the residence of the Tunis beys or traditional rulers – originally Ottoman Turks – until the French gave independence to the country in 1956. They were peaceably replaced in 1957 by the declaration of the Republic, which ushered in the new political state. This is a dream of a building, its tiling, wood carvings and paintings exquisitely miniatured, its rooms so tiny, and its ceilings so high, that every room seems like a perfect jewel box.

I found the Foreign Minister to be an urbane and sophisticated man. Slim, with a finely modelled and sensitive face, and always a touch of weariness in his eyes, exquisitely dressed, with a kindly presence, Ben Yahia looks as though every appointment were a summit meeting in one of the world's capitals. Sitting behind his elegantly carved wooden desk, he began immediately making enticing political and philosophical statements. 'We are in a process of maturation in Tunisia,' he began. 'There cannot be instant democracy or instant human rights.' He paused, then voiced a phrase that would often come back to challenge the many purist ideas about 'perfect' development in the Western world. 'Democracy,' he said, 'is not instant coffee…' He continued, 'We are pragmatic, rational, and we are trying to reflect and find solutions. We are not doctrinaire. When we see failures or difficulties that cannot be solved, we think harder.'

He let the curious but revealing little sentence about 'instant coffee' and 'democracy' hang there. He did not need to elaborate. I understood what he was saying. Tunisia was challenging not only Third Worldism but both the Far Left/Marxist/socialist idea of overnight development through 'faith' (the true ideology of

Communism) as well as the predominant purist, utopian American idea of 'instant' multiparty democracy as the answer.

'First of all, we started with birth control,' he went on. 'It was written into our first plans. We have nine million people today – we can handle that.' Next, he talked about the ways in which they are strengthening Tunisian culture on every level, so that human beings do not become isolated and alienated from their society, and he described how every child is being educated. Finally, he talked about the unique structuring of the state. Debates on policy are held on every level, ideas and disputes are passed upwards, the political committee of the ruling party then recommends policy options to the president, and finally he decides upon them. 'Tunisia proceeds on what we call a dialogue of all the social forces in the country,' he went on, as we sipped small cups of delicious Arabic coffee. 'We know that it is essential to get to the 21st century with a balanced society in which extremist tendencies can be controlled by antibodies within society.

'We didn't win over fundamentalism in the '80s with machine guns. We went to the roots of the cause of the threat, to the rural areas, to the South, to the pockets of poverty. Our NGOs became active organisations in bolstering the government programmes – we have 9,000 NGOs. We believe in the continuity of modern society – we want a nation of modernity with authenticity. If you go too far from your roots, it can all backfire, and we are proud of our roots, our culture, our religion: Muslim, Mediterranean, African, Arab... We believe in moderation in all respects. If we have succeeded in Tunisia, it is because we have gone step by step. Remember, people need to digest reforms.'

I went next to see another of the respected sons of today's Tunisia, the world-renowned scholar and Minister of Culture, Abdelbaki Hermassi. A rugged, charming man, the French-educated Hermassi, who taught in France until he was called home to oversee the crucial area of culture, is a fount of ideas that never seem to stop flowing.

'It's obvious that all the "grand ideologies" are in crisis,' Dr. Hermassi began. 'Whether with pan-Arabism or pan-Islamism, it is clear we are living in a much more complex world and a time when people are not going for the simplest solutions. In this kind of post-ideological period, people will judge their leadership on the chances in life it offers them.' He then explained the special appeal and relevance of 'evolutionary democracy', sometimes called 'tutelary democracy' or 'authoritarian democracy', 'Either you're born into democracy or you have to make it happen,' he told me that first day. 'If you have to make it happen, you have to go step by step, and you only have so many years to do it. This is a regime that is also acutely aware of the country's vulnerabilities, of its limited resources and its powerful neighbours. It has to be wise, it does not believe that it has the space to make mistakes.

'Why is our leadership so good? Well, from the 19th century onwards, we had one of the most reforming élites in the world. Tunisia has always had to have good leadership because it's a small country, a country in which errors are fatal. So partly because of that, it was the first country to build unions, the first to negotiate a peaceful independence, the first to see the limits of the first nationalist generation, the first to feel the need to retool and restructure our politics and our economy because the 'national liberation' period was over.

'My analysis is that, with the colonisation of the Arab world from the 19th century onwards, there was an overflow of resentment towards the West that meant that attitudes towards modernity and the West have always been very ambivalent. It became very popular among Arab élites to conceive of modernity not for its own sake but as modernity against the West – in cultural, religious and value terms. Meanwhile, we didn't modernise against the West, but with the West. The West has the universalised modernity because it has the universalised civilization. I think that this point is being realised slowly, and we should really fight for this. It means encouraging a dialogue of cultures and reinterpreting Islamic tradition in the light of Western modernity.'

And what about today? He leaned back in his chair and thought for just a moment. 'People are realising more and more that Tunisia has started a process, that it is an example,' he answered. 'We have a process of democratisation that is irreversible. In fact, more and more countries are now saying to us, 'We want to do what Tunisia is doing…'

And Just What is Tunisia Doing?

By the turn of the 21st century, the statistics of the country were little less than stunning. Throughout the 1990s, Tunisia's growth rate was consistent, at between five and eight percent a year; high anywhere in the world, and particularly notable because it seldom lowered. Its poverty level systematically dropped every year, until it reached an amazing 4.2 percent in 2002. According to World Bank figures, fully two-thirds of the society was considered middle class, while 80 percent owned their own homes. The carefully monitored population rate, a workable nine million people by the end of the century and deliberately kept low in order for progress to take root, was the envy of the overly-populated countries of the Middle East, Asia and Latin America – by 2002, for example, there were 65 million people in Egypt, 32 million in Algeria, and 140 million in Pakistan. Forty percent of women were working freely in Tunisia, in jobs such as the police, as CEOs of major companies, as diplomats, film-makers and journalists – and just about everything else besides. Five million visitors a year made Tunisia one of the most desirable tourist targets of Europeans from all countries, and more than 2,000 foreign companies were actively and enthusiastically investing and producing in Tunisia, a country which has given them every protection and opportunity.

Visiting Tunisia in December 1998, the U.N. Secretary-General Kofi Annan praised the country as 'one of the few countries in the world that serves as an international model.' The World Economic Forum designated Tunisia as the 'most competitive economy in Africa.' And in June 1999, the World Bank director of operations for North Africa, Christian Delvoie, said that, 'Tunisia is clearly in the lead in terms of economic and social indicators in the Middle East and the North Africa region.' Noting that the economic reforms there had struck an appropriate balance between economic and social changes throughout the country, Delvoie then stated that, 'Tunisia has developed a very specific model of development, with a consensual approach between labour unions, private sector and the government that creates a gradual pace of economic reform and a steady opening up to the external world.'

But it was in the spring of 2002, in the months after the Middle East terrorist attacks on the World Trade Center in New York and on the Pentagon in Washington, that a report was released at the United Nations in New York that shocked the entire region and chagrined most of its governments. As a result of this report, Tunisia and its 'way' suddenly stood out dramatically. The *Arab Human Development Report 2002, Creating Opportunities for Future Generations* was published by the U.N. Development Programme and the Arab Fund for Economic and Social Development, and was written largely by Arab intellectuals themselves – and it was a shocker. It uncovered findings that I had already written about: the fact, for example, that only four percent of the investment money of the entire world goes into the Middle East, including Israel; that huge numbers of young men are coming out of the schools and universities of the Middle East with nothing to do, and thus either going onto the streets or into the mountains; that women's talents are being terribly wasted. In short, on every level the report concluded, the Arab and Muslim countries were woefully, shamefully behind: 'About 65 million adult Arabs are illiterate... the utilisation of Arab women's capabilities through political and economic participation remains the lowest in the world... the capacity of the state has fallen short of the requirement to foster rapid growth... growth in Arab countries has been seriously hampered by low and declining labour productivity... GDP in all Arab countries combined stood at $531.2 billion in 1999 – less than that of a single European country, Spain ($595.5 billion)...'

But when the report gives examples, whether in terms of any of the constituent indicators of modernisation – political stability, the rule of law, population control, government effectiveness, constituents of welfare, the regulatory burden, the levels of graft, governance reform or education – Tunisia was always at the top of the list or at the very least among the top five or six countries, usually along with Bahrain, Oman, Qatar and Jordan.

Then, on top of this came the Iraq war, and 'nation-building' was in fashion once again. But no-one knew how to do it. The United States marched into Baghdad victoriously and was promptly threatened with having its 'victory' rescinded because it thought that democracy would just suddenly burst forth, spontaneously, from the Iraqi people. Instead there was only chaos. They had not looked seriously at the 'countries that work' – generally small countries like Tunisia.

Even those who criticise Tunisian politics as being dominated by one single party admit that the country represents a rare model that works in the developing world because it fits together the economic, the cultural, the historical, the social and, although in a different manner than elsewhere, the political. All of the necessary components of a healthy national life constantly intertwine, integrate and interact as they have begun to build, consciously and in just a generation, the kind of responsible citizenry and representative state that it took four centuries to develop organically in the north of Europe.

How have they done this? What exactly is it that has 'worked' in Tunisia? And if it has worked, then why has it worked? These are critically important questions. But there is still one more question – is it a different country or not?

Some analysts insist that Tunisia is so different that it cannot be used as a model for anywhere else, and a whole school of historical thought has danced around these ideas. Some analysts have insisted that Tunisia is 'different' because it is essentially 'European'. It is true that certain important historical, military and ethnic boundaries of the country adhere, for instance, to the historical borders of the Roman Empire, and this is important – within limits.

But in truth, Tunisia is an amalgam of many peoples. It is in many ways a superstitious people, given to magic; the very word 'Africa' comes from the early Roman name for historic Tunisia, 'Ifriqiya', and the region was pivotal in the spread of Islam across the entire north and west of black Africa. The next man will argue that Tunisia is different because its form of Islam is more moderate, more temperate, more harmonious than the more warrior-like styles of the religion. This is true, but Tunisia has also been the scene of great battles of Islam and even during the 1980s it faced the near-destruction of its carefully-wrought polity by rabid Islamists.

Then someone might say, well, the people themselves are just more sweet-tempered – more 'light blooded' – than the other Arabs. There is truth in that, too. But remember that the legendary Phoenician city of Carthage, with its bustling shipping port and its prosperous commercial houses, once stood on the northern coast on the outskirts of today's Tunis, and ruled all or part of the world for no less than 1600 years. The Romans were not light-blooded when they destroyed the most glorious city in the world in 146 BC, after ten days of ferocious fighting. Only a few foundation blocks and broken pillars remain of the city that the Romans destroyed, and the land that they salted so that it would never again return to life. The very word 'Carthage' has come to mean the total and irredeemable destruction of a civilisation and culture. In the movie *Patton*, General George Patton stands on the ruins of 1945 Europe, recalls the ancient city and murmurs, 'I have been here before.'

Still others will explain Tunisia's special development in terms of its beautiful landscape, and the way in which the land influences its people. But Tunisia is also a harsh land, with its chotts and deserts and steppes. Some in the élitist French Marxist and Far Left press in Paris will say that Tunisia only looks prosperous, that its surface prosperity is based upon a repressive government that allows no real deviation from the one-party line and no real journalistic freedom. Yet today, almost every Tunisian has a satellite dish on his roof, elections are held regularly and foreign newspapers, television, and the Internet are available almost everywhere, while five million tourists, from Europe, roam the country every year, peering into every corner.

I came to the conclusion that, while the country has made extraordinary leaps forward since its independence from France in 1956, it was the crucial 15 years from 1987 to 2002 that have secured Tunisia's place in the modern era as a country that is piecing itself together into a dynamic, thriving society.

I began to think of Tunisia in terms of a new kind of adventure. Explorers of old, like Marco Polo in the 13th century and Ibn Battuta, the Moroccan 'Prince of Travellers' in the 14th century, wandered the world creatively, in order to see with their own eyes the unknown societies, cultures and peoples beyond Europe, and to bring that knowledge back home with them. I began to think that what is needed today is a new kind of journey to discover the systems and processes that illuminate how whole peoples and cultures modernise and evolve. Today's great adventure is exploring the changes inside societies.

I started to see Tunisia first and foremost simply as a country where the leadership, the cultural figures, the business people, the commercial corps, the women, the Muslim clergy and the workmen out on the roads, all applied themselves. Both the leaders and the people were willing to throw aside the self-defeating nationalism that had contorted so much of the Middle East, and to accept rational solutions in order to arrive at genuine and palpable accomplishments. They were willing, when needed, to accept half-solutions, and sometimes even half-freedoms in the short term, so that they could evolve towards a full social, economic and political solution, and find a true and balanced national and personal independence in the long term.

'We don't have oil,' a wise Tunisian once said to me. 'We are lucky. Because the "oil mentality" creates a margin for squandering and risk, a mentality that is not pragmatically oriented, that does not produce and that creates an entire class of people who think they don't have to do anything.'

In the end, I knew that it didn't really matter whether the Tour de France ever actually came. I knew by then that what mattered most was that Tunisians like this young man, in contrast to much of the world around them, perceive their future as a series of open roads, some marked and some as yet unmarked. In such a world, it would clearly be unseemly not to have neat white lines down the centres of your roads.

What mattered, and what began to define the entire Tunisian experiment for me, was the fact that the Tunisians would certainly be ready for the Tour de France if and when it came.

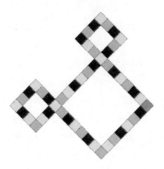

2. A Mosaic of a Land: *Politics by Stages*

'We are strong because we are moderate.'

Habib Bourguiba

The Man they Called the Supreme Combatant

Endless tales weave themselves around the life and spirit of the founder of modern Tunisia, Habib Bourguiba. All of them are revealing and many are amusing. There is the story of how, after he was president of the country, Bourguiba refused to let the ambassador from the Ivory Coast retire because it would mean the Soviet ambassador would automatically become dean of the diplomatic corps – and Bourguiba hated the Communists. Everyone remembers how he loved to tell his people not only how to act politically, but how to live, what to eat, how to control their children and even what colours should be used in public housing projects (always blue and white, in case you wondered).

But there was one story that I heard over and over again on my trips to Tunisia which best captured his unquenchable spirit. Sometimes Bourguiba is talking to the King of Morocco, sometimes to a Palestinian in Paris, sometimes to an audience in Tunisia. Someone poses an intriguing question to him: 'Aren't you afraid to educate your Tunisian "children"? Aren't you afraid that, once they are educated, they will turn against you?' And Bourguiba responds, with his accustomed wit and his easily-aroused anger: 'I would rather be thrown out by educated men than rule over jackals.'

In fact, it doesn't really even matter whether the story is true or not because what it reveals about his character was exactly on course. He meant those words, my God, how he meant them!

When you talk to Tunisians today about the 'Father of our Country' or the 'Supreme Combatant' or sometimes the 'Presidential Monarch', all of which he was alternately called, they often remember first the most vivid things about him. 'He loved to dance,' one young Tunisian dancer told me, pleased about it of course. 'He set up almost a culture of dance.' A young female artist remembered that, 'he adored women, he recited poems, he could be very humorous.' A Western diplomat who had known him in Tunis in his early days recalled the image Bourguiba projected, saying, 'He had great energy... he was a great orator... he loved his people... he would tour the country and crowds would gather everywhere for his two-hour speeches.' He was a dominating figure, filled with passion and conviction, whether he was in a Saharan jail, living on the Left Bank in Paris, studying at university in France, struggling in the underground, declaring independence or, finally, luxuriating at one of his presidential palaces after independence. He was a handsome man, small and agile, his face thin with high cheekbones that gave him the quizzical, logical look of the aristocrat-intellectual, but it was his eyes that always captured people's attention – they were sensuous and filled with amusement and expectation. Modesty was not a word that one would ever use to describe him.

Once, asked about the Tunisian system, he proclaimed grandly, but at the same time without pretension, as though he was simply speaking a given truth: 'I am the system!'

Yet despite this pride, and even though he spent nearly two decades of his life shifting between one French jail or another, there was also an attractive lightness about him. The famed 'light blood' of the Tunisian had come to course most eloquently through the veins of this remarkable, serious man. The pictures we have of him, however, show us a very different image.

Early in his life as a struggling student and a political prisoner, the pictures show a dark-haired man with a scrawny, often tormented face, his eyes staring straight ahead into the distance. Later, when he was in the midst of the independence struggle and always dressed meticulously, he became a strikingly handsome, polished, forceful young gentleman-agitator. Once he became President, his hair greying and now grandly dressed, he looked every bit the statesman or occasionally like some kind of modern monarch. Over those years, his image became transformed from that of a poor Tunisian to an Arab-French lawyer to a new free Tunisian, almost as if he carried the experience of his people within his own self. And he was always wise enough to know how to enjoy life to the fullest.

Habib Bourguiba was born in 1902 or 03 in Monastir in the independent-minded Sahel region. He was the eighth child of a family of only modest origins – and with him was born the independence movement. His father was a pensioner of the Bey's army, the local sheikh of a quarter in Monastir and the owner of a few olive trees. There was little evidence of the rebel in his early life, but young Habib was always an avid student and excelled at learning. It does seem from the testimonies of a number of people in whom he confided, that his awareness of social injustice was naturally instilled by experiences within his own family life, particularly regarding the experiences of the women.

His maternal grandmother, he related, had been divorced by her husband because she once served him his meal cold. She suffered direly for the rest of her life. His own mother died early, he told the American population advisor Elizabeth Maguire in 1981, because of the pain and stress of bearing so many children. 'Women can never enjoy full freedom and a chance to determine their own future until they are given complete control over their own bodies,' he told her. But Bourguiba was never simply an idealist. He saw women's emancipation not only as a matter of rights, but took into account the undeniable fact that, after all, women could earn as well as men for their families – and, not unimportantly, for the country.

But it was in Tunis, in a remarkable school that exemplified the profound changes that the country was already experiencing, that the young Habib began his true learning. It was when he moved from his first schools in Monastir to Sadiki College – founded by the Tunisian reformers in 1875 and still standing today on Casbah Square as the educational firmament of reformed education in Tunisia – that he confronted all the currents of reform, change and transition that were already throbbing through Tunisian life. Unique in Tunisia even in that era was the fact that learning had already been separated from the mosque and placed squarely in the hands of the state. In the heady and confident atmosphere of the times, Sadiki College found one of its most avid spirits in the searching mind and soul of young Habib Bourguiba. It was also in those years at Sadiki, and later in France, that he began to realise that mass education was a valuable tool, in part to forge a sense of national unity but also in order to create a supply of skilled workers capable of creating the kind of national development that he envisioned.

From his studies there, the young Habib travelled to France, where he studied law and political science, lost himself in French philosophy in the Latin Quarter and, so they say, even learned to dance the Charleston. He took a beautiful young Frenchwoman as his wife and soon had a son. He had lived with his wife before marriage and she was pregnant when they married; it was with admiration, but also astonishment, that his comrades at the university pointed to the fact that he wed her, when he did not have to, and took her back to Tunisia in 1927. Such an astonishing act had surely to be a mark of his noble character!

When you look at Bourguiba's actions during this era of the independence struggle, it seems on the surface that he was the exact replica of others of his 'independence generation' in the Third World, and that his trajectory to power was uncannily similar to that of the others'. He helped found a young independence group called the 'Young Tunisians', he started a movement newspaper, *L'Action Tunisienne*, he broke with the old-family, formal, élitist old Destour or Constitution Party and started a new party, the Neo-Destour, which more truthfully represented the independence fighters and agitators. He and his dedicated group of young recruits were soon travelling to every village to talk to the people, to convince them, and always to organise them.

Soon the party had recruited 100,000 members from a population of two million people. They did not, as in most cases of national development at that time, only come from one small revolutionary bund but from all walks of life. The Neo-Destour was made up of intellectuals and small business people, farmers, workers and women and, in those early days, despite the party's origins as a modern and secular party, Bourguiba was sagacious enough never to deliberately antagonise the religious and conservative circles. From the end of World War Two until 1951, the party was organised in a pyramidal structure, with branches or cells at the bottom of the pyramid and federations at the provincial level, which in turn chose delegates to the national party congresses and also elected representatives to the highest body, the National Congress. From the Congress was chosen a political bureau with ten members who essentially ran the party. But although that structure was common at the time, there were dramatic differences in the Tunisian experience from the start. The structure of the Neo-Destour would serve as a model for the early Tunisian single-party state, but because of Bourguiba's particularist personality and outlook, it would also have flexibility and moderation built into it.

It was in the midst of these institutional arrangements that Tunisian women, drawing upon reformers and reform movements of the 19th century, began participating not only actively in politics, but also in actual street demonstrations as early as 1938 and then again in 1952. This was something that was quite simply unheard of in the Arab world.

The salon-Bourguiba could become the street fighter-Bourguiba when necessary, fomenting demonstrations on the streets of Tunisia. At one point, when he was in exile in 1952 and 53, he even organised guerrillas (*fellaghas* in Arabic) who were ready to take to the hills in all-out war, causing the French to send 70,000 troops to Tunisia, which were still not enough to repulse Bourguiba's 'troops'. In all, he spent the equivalent of ten years in prison before he saw his country freed in 1956.

Yet anyone who was studying him at all carefully would have looked at his Neo-Destour party and noted how very different everything that Habib Bourguiba laid his hand on was from the very beginning. Philosophically, even his party represented more a set of tactics than an ideology or even a political creed.

'The Neo-Destour represented a new method and a new kind of Tunisian nationalism,' William Spencer wrote perceptively in *The Land and People of Tunisia*. Essentially, he said, Bourguibism rested on the 'moral values of Western democracy', which Bourguiba believed in, yet it also borrowed the oriental system of bargaining, point by point, for every advantage. Bourguiba often compromised, but what his critics failed to understand was the fact that he also never surrendered. Actually, he was rather blunt about it. In a speech in 1961, Bourguiba said, 'Politics is the art of attaining the possible...' In point of fact, Bourguibism does not take what is offered and then ask for more. It accepts a partial compromise only insofar as it offers the possibility of taking everything.

Indeed, it was because of its pyramidal structure and because of the mass nature of the Neo-Destour, that the entire enterprise was spared disintegration under the French repression that was to come.

It was precisely in these years of the 1930s and '40s that the most extreme forms of nationalism were sweeping the Arab world, with the most radical philosophies and ideologies – Soviet Communist, Egyptian Nasserite, secular Syrian/Iraqi Ba'athist, Islamic Muslim Brotherhood, some enlightened autocracies – frenetically dominating the rhetoric and the stage. True to his egalitarian spirit, Bourguiba disliked them all almost equally. Unlike the other Third World leaders, he wanted to build productive farms and not unproductive, oversized steel mills. He wanted to free the mind, even of the very poorest, albeit of course under his direction; and despite his lavish lifestyle later in life when his dreams had been realised, he truly saw his rule as empowering his people economically, socially and eventually politically – even if, as in the famous story about his not wanting to 'rule over jackals', they might turn out to be the ones to overthrow him.

Bourguiba particularly disliked the Communists – perhaps even 'hated' is not too strong a word for his feelings towards them. He felt that the Communists lived only to divide people, and that was not his mission. Nationalism in Tunisia under Habib Bourguiba was never going to be subsumed by some damned internationalist Marxist movement! He was a man of specificity and of possibility, not of diffuse and grandiose plans about things that could never be. In Tunisia, he averred repeatedly, people have no attraction to world citizenship for its own sake. In *Bourguiba's Tunisia*, Pierre Rossi wrote perceptively that, 'In Bourguiba's eyes, any struggle for liberation has the nation as its basis...' As to the Tunisian population, it was 'one of the least metaphysical peoples in the world and, if it cares for anything, it is above all reality.' Tunisians had the 'mentality of gardeners', he wrote, without any intent to insult but only to indicate that they live to sow and reap creatively, rather than to pull up and destroy. Having that mentality, 'they could hardly fail to appreciate the architectural order and peace of Bourguiba's work.'

Far from the Communists' adopted credo that 'the end justifies the means', Bourguiba simply adapted moral ends to the means. You might say that, for him, only the means justified the means and only the end justified the end.

The brilliant Iraqi-born historian Majid Khadduri wrote particularly sensitively of Bourguiba, whom he knew, in his book, *Arab Contemporaries: The Role of Personalities in Politics*, in which he considered the nature of Bourguiba's curious and unresolved relations with the other Arab leaders. Bourguiba stood 'almost unique among contemporary Arab leaders because of his use of political methods which, though acceptable to his followers, have aroused grave concern in other quarters,' he wrote. 'These methods have brought him into sharp conflicts with other Arab leaders, despite the fact that the goals which he sought to achieve for his country were not essentially different from the goals of other Arab countries. He was denounced by Arab nationalists, including even some moderate leaders, as a tool of imperialism, and by revolutionary leaders as a traitor to Arab nationalism.'

Why, he then asked, 'was Bourguiba's image so tarnished in contemporary Arab eyes and what was the real man?' He concluded that, 'Bourguiba's political approach has been to achieve national goals by the method of "gradualism", a step-by-step process in which each step is designed to break new ground and lead to the next logical step until his countrymen are eventually set along the path of normal progress that has been established by advanced nations. This method, according to Bourguiba is a perpetual "struggle for positions". As he explained it to me, when the first position is won, it must be consolidated before the next is undertaken... Thus the perennial struggle towards national goals must proceed.'

To think therefore, that he was only 'moderate' – he himself had written in his own book, *Mission*, that, 'We are strong because we are moderate' – would be a treacherous oversimplification. For he used his time very specifically and always in order to gain what he wanted in the end. He seemed to realise instinctively, as many radical Arab leaders did not, that if you mobilise people, as he did so brilliantly, you risk all by having them awaken at the end of the day with nothing in their hands or hearts.

Bourguibism would come over the years to be called 'evolutionary change', or 'politics by stages', or a 'strategy based on realism'. In truth, in terms of tactics, he was a Tunisian Machiavelli, but one with a high moral compass in terms of his strategic objectives. 'Such a policy is fully justified when the ideal solution is not immediately feasible,' Bourguiba himself wrote in *Foreign Affairs* in an article called 'The Tunisian Way' in April 1966. But then, typically, he warned that, 'it must always be dynamic, each step preparing the way for the next step to follow.'

He was a political genius when it came to seeing, grasping and then employing (greatly to his benefit) local crises to make his point. When one of his most trusted lieutenants, Salah Ben Youssef, influenced by Nasserite Arabism, challenged Bourguiba's patient, often frustrating step-by-step liberation of Tunisia and called for instant, full independence from France, in what came to be called the 'Youssefist Rebellion', Bourguiba used the occasion to warn the French that he could not resist the extremists for much longer. Of course, he got what he wanted.

Part of the French salon-Bourguiba loved to discuss and negotiate. Yet few around him in those heady days realised that he always tried to grasp and comprehend his opponent's situation and psychology for his and his country's own benefit. French salon-Bourguiba never stopped negotiating, not as long as there was a thread of hope. His was a method that was constantly being refined, even as the country, by the 1940s, seemed to be slipping into French hands. He had not only to fight the French, but stop them from assimilating the Tunisians or there would be no Tunisia, in his terms, at all. In 1932, when assimilation looked to be a real threat, Bourguiba got a learned Muslim sheikh to declare that any Muslim who died as a French national had lost his right to be buried in a Muslim ceremony, which cannily posited tradition and belonging against fear of anomie and lostness. He was fighting extreme modernism and paralysing fatalism at the same time.

Despite his conflicts with the French during World War Two, when the Axis and then the Allies swept across North Africa, with Tunisia the pivot of some of the worst fighting in February 1943, he allied his movement firmly with the French and never for a moment wavered in this position. (Of course, he also saw the Allies as the clear victors.) And once the war was over, as he had foreseen, there was such an air of 'liberation, now!' in the air, in a world rapidly becoming euphorically post-colonial, that it was only a matter of time before Tunisia would gain its independence.

Prof. L. Carl Brown, Princeton scholar and one of the major authorities on Tunisia and its leader, wrote of Bourguiba that his 'philosophy' was, 'in fact, uncommon good sense presented with deceptive simplicity and clarity – rather like the common sense of a Machiavelli, a Montesquieu or a Madison.' He ticked off the essential characteristics of Bourguibism: '1) Avoid self-deception. Do not seek refuge in an unreal golden age when "we" were strong or civilised and "they" weak or barbaric. 2) Explain the true situation to your followers, without lapsing into emotionally satisfying but politically damaging scapegoatism. 3) Have clear long-term goals but always be willing to reach them in stages. 4) Seek not so much to defeat your opponent as to win over your opponent. 5) Be tactically flexible. This includes not only showing a willingness to accept half a loaf for the time being, but also a willingness to risk confrontation against a stronger opponent in order, ultimately, to show that you will fight if forced to do so, thereby avoiding the stigma of being seen as weak on time, long on speeches but short on organisational muscle and will... 6) Be rational and far-sighted in setting policies. Do not let your very human desire to lash out at the enemy presently inflicting harm and humiliation, cause you to misread the utility for your purpose of that enemy's enemies.'

Bourguiba was in his prison cell on the Ile de Groix off the coast of Brittany, when the new Premier of France, Pierre Mendès-France made a sudden flight to Tunis in 1954 and offered the Tunisians 'Home Rule'. That was not enough, but Bourguiba knew that it was now only a matter of time; his tactics and his strategies had worn the French down point by point. He and his men and women had brilliantly ridden the waves of change in the world, and were now sailing victoriously to shore.

In the end, Bourguiba led a movement and then a country which was the only one in the region to make a really successful transition from colonialism to a sovereign nation, from traditionalism to reasonable modernism. He was the only one who did not substitute ever more extremist nationalist rhetoric for palpable accomplishments and the only one who, after the glorious early days of independence, went on to lay the basis for producing and building a modern state.

When the Supreme Combatant returned victoriously to the country in 1955, the Tunisians danced in the streets and toasted their hero with delicate-flavoured brandy made from Cap Bon figs, while the veiled women let loose with their ear-splitting and ululating cries. By March 1956, a new treaty was signed in Paris, invalidating the Bardo Treaty of 1881 which had created the French Protectorate. Tunisia was recognised as a sovereign state whose government would now be a constitutional monarchy under the bey. But it was clear that even this arrangement was part of the past and was not going to last; and so in 1957 the bey was deposed and Habib Bourguiba, ever and always the Supreme Combatant, became the first president of his country.

Patient, but disinclined to waste his time, Bourguiba then proclaimed to a correspondent, 'I invented Tunisia.' And to a great degree, he had. But perhaps he had also done something more. He had introduced into the Middle Eastern and Arab world an entirely new approach to historical development and, in doing this, he had first to draw upon every single epoch of the rich and complex saga that is the history of Tunisia.

In less complex countries, you can often draw clear, straight lines from one people to the next and from one era to the next. You can relate families and generations in a more or less straight line and trace the names, the customs and the heritage down through the ages, one after the other. But Tunisia is not that kind of country. Tunisia's story is not so much a linear one but rather a mosaic, with separate pieces patiently and artistically pieced together, and stories woven to form the larger picture.

Historians trace the art of the mosaic to the 8th century BC when Greek artists worked first with tiny pieces of pebble, then stone, and finally glass. The mosaic artist does not have the usual range of colours available to the artist, because each piece has its own, solid colour. The artist has to achieve the same variation of light and shadow as is possible in painting through the complex artistry of blending pieces, already coloured, into what appears from a distance to be one shaded, shadowed and illuminated whole. It was under Rome that mosaics came exquisitely into their own, and in Tunisia today, travellers come from all over the world to see the famous Bardo Museum in Tunis, a former royal palace, containing room after room of precious mosaics which lay out in breathtaking detail the ambitions (many), cruelties (more than enough) and passions (positively vast in number) of the cultures of Tunisia.

How amazing that the social mosaic of Tunisia over so many centuries should turn out to be every bit as complex and rich as the artistic mosaics of stone and glass that underlie the country!

The Roman Structure

If one had to choose a single period of Tunisia's history that has most formed and influenced the country and laid the foundations for its early development and spirit – and eventually for the spirit of Bourguibism – that period would be the Roman one. The Romans swept across the Mediterranean, destroying great Carthage in fields of flame in the three bloody Punic Wars, and then stayed for more than 500 years, from 146 BC to 439 AD. Building upon the same rich hills and seaside as the original Carthaginian or Punic Carthage – and certainly on the foundations of the same city that they had so cruelly wiped off the face of the earth the year the Roman legions came – Rome went on to build 200 cities across North Africa, maintaining the centre of the 'Provincia Africana' in what was Roman Carthage and what is today modern Tunis.

As she did everywhere, Rome imposed her will first through her physical imprint, constructing thousands of miles of roads with mileposts marking every 1,000 paces or every 4,584 feet, stately public buildings that were sometimes as high as seven storeys, aqueducts, bridges, dams, irrigation systems, temples, baths and aristocratic homes. Illustrating once again their amazing engineering talents, the Romans created one aqueduct, in the area of Zaghouan, which carried 8.5 million gallons of water daily to Carthage. Roman Carthage soon became the granary of the Roman Empire, and no fewer than 15 percent of Rome's senators came from Tunisia.

In the end, Rome and her civilised habits were so dominant and so attractive that even when the northern European Vandals – a wild people not exactly known for their fine manners – invaded in 439 AD, within 80 years they were wearing togas, enjoying the beautiful Roman mosaics and behaving like, well, Romans. And who could blame them?

If you go to the ruins of Dougga in north-western Tunisia today, you can easily get an idea of the grandeur that characterised this empire of Rome and understand how it was that this period provided the first basis for the modern institutions of Tunisia. Even today, the golden ruins are breathtaking. Dating from 46 BC, they spread over a large mountain top and dip down into the fertile valleys of Tunisia, filled with olive groves, and pomegranate, almond and peach trees. An exquisite theatre was opened in 168 AD under the Roman Emperor and philosopher Marcus Aurelius, whose reign from 161 to 180 AD laid the basis for the Golden Age of the Roman Empire. It dominates the hilltop where the Greek tragedies were performed, just a few miles away from the 'shadow zone beyond the Roman settlement', where the 'primitive' Berber tribes could only watch on the sidelines of what were then, effectively, the borders of Rome.

For if this territory of Rome was part of Europe, it was also part of Africa. Even the settlers adopted local habits, like hating the wind from the west, considering it either too hot or too cold, and believing that everything that comes from the west is bad. This idea apparently stems from early experiences of invasions from that direction. In fact, in the open temple square of Dougga, there still stands a round metal sundial with the indicators of north, south, east and west. Whether

Roman or Islamic, all of the great squares had sundials, perhaps because they were never sure which way the wind was blowing.

But there was another, darker side to the Roman Empire. As graceful and amenable as these beautiful and weathered old Roman ruins at Dougga are, just as frightening are other remnants of the age. This side can be seen most disturbingly in El Djem, the giant and, at least to me, terrifying Roman amphitheatre in the centre of the country, which happened also to be the third largest Roman coliseum in the empire after Rome and Capua.

The ruins rise today like a spectral invader over a peaceful and abundant land. Dark red in colour, with vast and rough stone, El Djem is like a terrible, bloody scar on the landscape. Its partially-destroyed sides rise up in jagged, broken shards to the sky. The floors are open and the visitor can look directly down into the underground caverns and halls, where the wild animals of Africa (lions, bears and tigers) were brought to tear apart Christians and others, all to the thunderous applause of the crowds. Roman Africa, like the rest of the Roman Empire, was cruel as well as custodial, but one must remember that many scholars thought Carthage had been just as cruel.

I came to the conclusion that the reason why the amphitheatre seemed to be so unpityingly truthful was because it rose up so suddenly, all of itself, out of the calm and simple beauty of the Tunisian countryside. In other Roman cities, institutions like the courts, the public buildings and the temples diffused the dark power of such buildings, but at El Djem there were no longer any surrounding structures that could absorb the cold cruelty of the place. The original city had fallen to dust over the centuries and had been replaced with a typical, amenable blue and white Tunisian town. Today the amphitheatre is a stage for international arts events, including a classical music festival.

It was in those same centuries that the Romans effectively set out the boundaries of their rule, and thus of fledgling Europe's rule across North Africa. After the capture and destruction of Carthage in 146 BC, the Romans installed a huge demarcation border ditch – the *fossa regia* it was called in Latin – that runs from Tabarka on the north-west coast, to the south and then eastward to Thaenaes, south of Sfax, the commercial and port city that sits about halfway down the eastern coastline. Robert D. Kaplan, an American journalist and historian who has made his name travelling to the ends of the earth writing about the roots of cultural history, has analysed perceptively that the *fossa regia* delineated the lines of European cultural influence and expansion; lines which still make some sense today.

The African Rome also had its Christian period, and even today, archaeologists are discovering Christian catacombs dug deep in the rocky terrain of Tunisia. After the Roman Emperor Constantine was converted to Christianity in 313 AD and Rome took Christianity as its state religion, Carthage became the seat of the bishopric where the famous Saint Augustine studied and wrote his *City of God*, asserting that we are all only temporary travellers in an earthly world. North African Christianity was often in ferment both intellectually and politically, torn in a struggle between the Church of Rome and various odd anti-Catholic movements, the most important being the Donatist heresy that swept across eastern North Africa in the 4th century AD and stands as an early form of anti-foreign nationalism. This piece of the Tunisian mosaic was characterised by every kind of intellectual debate, and by its sheer energy. The Christians there had spirit – in those early years, the bishops of Roman Carthage even dared to correct the Popes in Rome!

Finally, the Roman struggle over Tunisia also formed the man who is today considered the archetypal hero of Tunisia, the general they still respect, and call only 'Hannibal'. For North African Rome was not moulded out of ancient Carthage without bloodshed. First, three terrible Punic Wars had to be fought between the Carthaginians and Romans from 264 to 146 BC. Those wars ended with the fall of Carthage, but they are remembered for the mounted cavalcade led by Hannibal from Spain, across the Pyrenees and the Alps, and down through Italy to the very gates of Rome, beginning years of warfare.

What remains in most readers' minds, and hardly surprisingly so, is the fact that Hannibal journeyed with 58,000 African, Spanish, Ligurian, Gaulish, Punic, Italian, and Greek troops and no fewer than 37 elephants, which historians believe were a native African species. It was clearly one of history's most extraordinary journeys, for man and beast alike.

Hannibal, like so many of the peoples and historic figures who had come to that special part of Africa, was a seeker. He studied textbooks of leadership by Greek tutors, including Alexander the Great, and had some military experience in Spain. He was unusually close to his soldiers, a fact made more extraordinary given that most of them were mercenaries. It shows the degree to which the Northern Africans could adapt their manners and ways to varied and very different peoples. He was also a great risk taker and a man of legendary courage. The distinguished Roman historian Livy, who lived between 64 BC and 17 AD, drew a portrait of him unusual for an intellectual at the service of a subject's enemy: 'Never has a soul swayed more supplely between two more opposing qualities: subordination and command... No other chief could inspire his soldiers with more confidence, more daring... No fatigue could wear out his body, nor break his spirit... He could often be seen lying on the ground amongst the sentinels and guards covered with a soldier's tabard...'

Livy was no idle admirer; he also wrote that Hannibal exemplified, 'excessive cruelty, a more than Punic perfidy,' and that, 'nothing was true, nothing was sacred for him, he did not fear the gods, did not respect the sermons, had no religion.'

Yet when the warrior returned from his defeat outside Rome – the fearsome cry in the walled cities under his attack having been, 'Hannibal at the Gates!' – the general then applied his gifts to civic society. 'He used the military to make political changes,' the Tunisian historian Dr. Nejib Ben Lazreg told me the day we visited Dougga. 'He was ingenious because the military was made up of different nationalities. What does he represent today? A man who accepted the challenge! After the war ended, he tried to reform the institutions, to improve the situation of farmers, to control the aristocracy and to reduce taxes. He signed a peace treaty which gave Spain and parts of North Africa to the Romans. Finally he left secretly and for a time went to Bithynia in what is today Turkey. He committed suicide there, rather than be captured by the Romans.'

It seemed to me that, despite the fact that he actually lost the second Punic War, Hannibal is honoured in modern Tunisia quite simply because he was not an oversimplified ancient 'hero' but a complex modern figure. Despite his strength and cunning Hannibal was, in many ways, a curiously ambivalent figure. The colours in the mosaic of his personality range from the bold ones of blood and conquest that surrounded the old Tunisia, to the more muted tones of civic and psychological development of the new.

The Arab Soul

If you wish to see the symbol of the next major period of the formation of Tunisia, the Arab conquest, particularly the beauty of the gracious and softened part of Islam that it sometimes carried with it, you need to go to what is unquestionably Tunisia's favourite spot, the magical white and blue village of Sidi Bou Said on the hills of Carthage. Jutting out into the sea just outside Tunis, the little city seems to be a kind of sentinel searching the sky for travellers from outside – and, how eager they all were to come! The Crusader king, Saint Louis – Louis IX of France – came to 'Sidi Bou' in 1270 AD to conquer and, so the story goes, ended up being enchanted by a beautiful Berber princess and living his last years in happy idleness amidst the beauty. More certain are the stories of how famous writers such as Guy de Maupassant and André Gide, along with artists like Auguste Macke and Paul Klee, so loved the place.

When you approach it from the sea, Sidi Bou, as it is familiarly called, is like a white mirage, shimmering on the top and sides of a cliff. When you approach it from the land, the town is like a delicate white hand pointing to the sea. Once inside, you find yourself in an exquisite village with studded blue Arabic carved doorways and cafés overflowing with flowers.

Sufism came to fruition here in a perfect physical example of the kindness and generosity that can be juxtaposed against the war-like qualities of martial Islam. The salt breeze seems to blow fresher here than anywhere else in Tunisia, perhaps because of the haunting Andalusian songs that sing of the 'lost kingdom' of Moorish Spain across the sea, or perhaps because of the famous *marabout* or holy man who, it was said, could cure rheumatism and malaria and order the scorpions to unsheathe their stings.

Consider the very word, 'marabout', with its artistic sound. It can mean 'little saint' but it can also refer to the saints' domed and pristinely white little tombs that grace the arms of the hills all across Tunisia. These marabouts of Sufism gave people a respite from the unforgiving 'oneness' of God – in them and in their tombs, one could find intimacy with God and, in these diminutive monuments to everyday good men, face not only the authority of the eternal but the truest comradeship of the human world.

On my last trip to Tunisia I climbed up to see the tomb of the town's famous *marabout*, Sidi Bou Said Al Beji. The tomb sits up two flights of steep stairs from the famous Café des Nattes, the most popular in town. It is a small, perfectly neat white cluster of small patios and small rooms, one of which holds his casket. It is on the highest point above the sea and clearly a splendid place to meditate or think.

'He was a pious man, a holy man,' my guide was saying of the marabout whose special spirit infuses modern Tunisia today. 'He used to pray a lot and read the Koran. He studied theology in Morocco and then he moved to Tunis, in part because of the reformist behaviour of our people. In 603, he lived in Mecca for three years, and went to Syria and sat with the Muslim leaders, where knowledge was passed on to other sheikhs and theologians like the sufi sages. He died in 689 AD... during sunset prayers.' In short, it had been left to the Arab conquest to give the Tunisians the basis for their spiritual life and their soul.

Towards the middle and end of the 7th century, after the death of the Prophet Mohammed, the Muslim Arabs swept without warning out of the deserts of Arabia, westward across North Africa. Seemingly overnight, they took most of North Africa and the Maghreb, even settling as far as Southern Spain. Once again, the original Berber people of Tunisia were the most difficult to vanquish. They held out bravely but hopelessly in their hillside fortresses along the cliffs of the desert south. The Arab-Islamic conquerors consolidated their hegemony in the area of modern-day Tunisia between 647 and 698 AD and then moved swiftly to Spain in 711. At this pivotal moment in history, Mohammed's idea of the One God, which had been awakened in him during his travels among Christians and Jews, spread to all of North Africa, sweeping away remaining pantheons of the many quarrelsome, love-making, treacherous, cruel and demanding gods of the Mediterranean world.

It was during this era that the gracious pilgrim city of Kairouan, the oldest Muslim city in North Africa, was built in central Tunisia in 670 AD, fully three centuries before the building of Cairo in Egypt. Its founding was typical of the practicality and balance that so often characterised Tunisia. Kairouan's founders deliberately placed it in the very centre of the country so that it would be one day's walk to the sea (to watch out for who was coming, especially the hated Byzantine fleet) and one day's walk to the mountains (where they could keep watch over the troublesome Berbers on their eternal mountainsides). It was a stable, prosperous, religious city, with strong walls and gates and a famous pool which assured the inhabitants of sufficient water.

One of the Prophet's companions, Abu Zamaa al Balawi, who was killed in a battle near Kairouan, is buried in the city. He was known as 'the Prophet's Barber', as it is said that he was buried with three hairs from the Prophet's beard which he kept with him during his lifetime. But before he died, at least so it is said, he had buried a piece of the Prophet's hair in the great mosque, where 9,000 worshippers knelt in prayer together and scribes copied books in both Arabic and Hebrew.

Kairouan was the pivot for the entire new conquest that was aimed not only northwards to Spain but also southwards to Africa. From Kairouan, the Muslims launched the conquests of Sicily, Malta and Granada in Spain, but also those of Niger, Mali and Nigeria in black Africa. Historic Carthage became an Arab city in 698 AD and slowly transformed itself into the modern city that would come to be known under the Hafsid dynasty as Tunis. Once again, Tunisians had to adapt to new institutions, or die. Under the Arabs, in place of Roman authority the new city-state was now ruled by an appointed Caliph, who was considered to be the direct successor and representative of the Prophet. It was then that the famous and beautiful Zeitouna or 'Olive Tree' in present-day Tunis became one of the great mosques of the world, housing 36,000 precious volumes and teaching children from all across this new North African Muslim Empire.

It was from his studies at Zeitouna that the accomplished and original 14th century Muslim philosopher Ibn Khaldun, broke the theological limits of religion and heritage to propound a 'science of culture' which became famous across the world and, not unimportantly, serves as a philosophical basis for Tunisia's development ideas today. Indeed, many historians crown him with the title of the 'Father of Sociology' or the 'First Sociologist'. Expounding a totally new cyclical theory of history long before the modern age, Ibn Khaldun was convinced that states, like human beings, go through cycles, perhaps lasting about 120 years, in which there are periods of youth, of virility, of maturity and of old age. In his *Muqaddimah* or *Prolegomena*, he showed an acute awareness of exactly the same interpenetration of cultures and civilisations that Tunisia had experienced, noting that while a conqueror sometimes destroys everything that came before him and imposes his own forms and patterns, the conqueror also frequently adopts the civilisation he has tried to vanquish, particularly if it is intrinsically superior to his own. This was, of course, pure Tunisian history.

Al Andalus: The Model of Liberal Islam

The next great period of Tunisia's history – the one that provides us with the very model of much of what the modern state is working towards today – was brought home to me poignantly on the day of modern Tunisia's fifth anniversary, November 7, 1992. Since it was my first trip to the country, and I had only barely touched its history, there was still plenty for me to be surprised about.

I was invited to the country's National Day reception in Carthage Palace, and here came dramatically up against the Moorish or, as the Moors in Spain were called, the 'Morisco' influence in Tunisia. We were chatting at the reception, when the moment came for President Zine El Abidine Ben Ali to enter the room. It was the first time I had seen him, and he entered elegantly, but not alone. In a moving circle, his cabinet surrounded him and all together they glided gracefully around the room. The circle protected him but also gave people the idea that everyone was being greeted personally by him. Even while enjoying this little scene, I suddenly felt that something was 'amiss', or that I was being plagued by a memory that refused to declare itself. I studied the situation more seriously. The President, like the other men, was wearing a flowing long robe, with dark stockings and a kind of Moroccan-style open shoe. The entire entourage represented an elegant moving drama. I had seen this entire style somewhere before – but where?

At that point, a European historian who had been standing next to me, noticed my puzzlement. 'Perhaps you didn't know?' he suggested kindly. 'Many of the Tunisians are descendants of the Moors. They came here after 1492 when Catholic Spain drove out the Moors and the Jews. That is why you recognise the costumes. They are not African or even Arab costumes, they are purely Moorish.'

Curiously enough on the same day, another aspect of the Middle East was represented there with Ben Ali, for next to him in the circle as it moved around the room, was Yasser Arafat, the head of the Palestine Liberation Organisation, whose offices had been in Tunisia since the early 1980s. The contrast between the two men could not have been more revealing of the many different sides of Arab or Muslim culture. Ben Ali had the elegance of all the cultures that had made up Tunisia, while Arafat, as always proudly unshaven and grimy, was dressed in a combat suit with a red and white *keffiyah* around his head. The handsome and meticulously appointed Ben Ali, his elegant Moorish robes recalling one of the greatest times in Muslim history, stood next to the region's pre-eminent liberation movement chieftain, with his other dimension and mosaic!

Soon after Islam came to Tunisia at the end of the 7th century AD with the conquest of the Berber south and the Carthaginian-Roman-Byzantine north, it quickly moved to southern Spain. In 711 AD, Arab Muslims led a Berber army across the Straits of Gibraltar and soon established across a half moon of southern Spain, the wondrous empire they called 'Al Andalus', which historians have called the 'ornament of the world'. There, for 780 years – longer than the span of the Roman Empire – there developed a Moorish Muslim state, with a caliphate based in Cordoba, the city that personified the apogee of the Moors' civilisation. The city's library housed some 400,000 volumes – more than ten times the number in the Zeitouna mosque in Tunis, whose library was already much revered, and at a time when the largest library in Christendom held books numbered only in the hundreds.

In that remarkable age, Jews, Christians and Muslims lived side by side in a culture of tolerance, progress and prosperity virtually unknown in the world of its age – or any other. The two great philosophers of the day were Maimonides the Jew, and Averroes the Muslim.

Writing of that unique moment in time, Maria Rosa Menocal wrote in her classic book, *The Ornament of the World: How Muslims, Jews and Christians Created a Culture of Tolerance in Medieval Spain*, 'Their illumination of the rest of the universe transcended differences of religion. It was in Al Andalus that the profoundly Arabised Jews rediscovered and reinvented Hebrew poetry. Much of what was created and instilled under Muslim rule survives in Christian territories, and Christians embraced nearly all aspects of Arabic style, from philosophy to architecture. Christian palaces and churches, like Jewish synagogues, were often built in the style of the Muslims, the walls frequently covered with Arabic writing; one synagogue in Toledo even includes inscriptions from the Koran...'

Astonishingly, the philosophers of this era, 'saw no contradiction in pursuing the truth, whether philosophical or scientific or religious, across confessional lines.' In the end, 'much of Europe, far beyond the Andalusian world, was shaped by the vision of complex and contradictory identities that was first made into an art form by the Andalusians.'

But the Catholics in Spain began to strike back. In 1248, they took Granada and by 1492 they had expelled the Jews of Spain and many of the Moors. The Jews spread across the world, to Turkey, Greece, Italy and to some of the Arab countries. But most of the Moors who fled Spain under the Inquisition between 1492 and 1611 went to Tunisia or other North African countries. It was a huge and rich emigration. More than 100,000 Moors fled the 'Reconquista' in Spain, and they carried their richly-developed culture with them. It was a culture that already blended European-Christian, Arabic-Islamic and Islamic-Jewish traditions, and it strongly influenced Maghrebi society. Many of the upper and middle class refugees entered government service, both in the military and the civilian bureaucracies, while artisans from Andalusia, which is still the name of the southern region of Spain, immensely enriched the commercial life of North African society. That tolerant, brilliant culture gave much to Tunisia, even as its brilliance was becoming lost to Spain.

Skilled Andalusian artisans created a remarkably high level of affluence in Tunisia. The Andalusians formed guilds of potters, weaver, dyers, and *chechia*-makers, and in the various quarters of Tunis, as the city expanded beyond its walled medina, the guilds brought a distinctive style of their own; bold black and white striped mosques, religious schools and palaces, and fountains for public drinking water. A walk through Tunis' charming, clean and evocative medina today carries you back into another world.

Dating from the 7th century AD, the medina is a world of small souqs, whose sheer variety seems to parallel the myriad different peoples who have journeyed through Tunisia. The souqs of what are known as the 'noble guilds' include the perfumers' souq (el Attarine), the booksellers' souq (el Koutbia), the jewellers' souqs (el Berka) the Turkish souq (el Trouk) and the fez makers' souq (ech Chaouachia). They are all evidence of the proud and noble specialisation of the early craftsmen of the region.

Unlike modern cities, where streets are generally laid out and marked with practical efficiency, the medinas of the Middle East are invitations to the unexpected. At any moment there will appear from nowhere a tiny byway that you never expected, with charming, secretive coffee houses and shops whose fronts seem modest and prim, but whose inner rooms are as elegant as palaces. Mirrors soldered in beautifully hammered silver reflect from shop to shop, just as the different cultures of Tunisia reflect back and forth upon one another. Many of the traders in the medina have created wonderful terraces on their roofs, often adorned with intricately-painted ceramic tiles, so that their clients can escape the shadows and the close air of the medina and luxuriate in views of the rooftops and the beautiful pinnacles of the minarets.

These men and women of ancient Tunisia were never part of an overweaning, powerful economic state, doomed to become engulfed in huge and process-ridden bureaucracies. Whether they were Arab, or Jewish, whether Turkish or Hafsid or Almohad, all were craftsmen in the most precious sense of the word. They lived for their craft and their craft defined them. Those with high artistic capacity and quality were revered, and the others gained – and were not diminished, as is so often the case today – by the others' excellence. That is why, in so many places in Tunisia, one can suddenly find some small miracle of artistry, the result of a hand of excellence preserved and nurtured over many centuries.

The Islamic Reform

By the end of the 20th century, one of the great preoccupations of the Western world was the question of Islamic reform. By that time, a small percentage of the Muslim world, which by then constituted no less than one-fifth of the entire population of mankind, had become involved in radical, fundamentalist terrorism.

At first the terror was directed at the moderate Arab governments – primarily Egypt, Algeria, and Jordan as well as Tunisia. Then the target turned towards the West, and in particular the United States. The Second Intifada raged in Israel and Palestine, with the very real danger of a total breakdown in the Middle East. The American administration talked ceaselessly about invading Iraq in order to remove weapons of mass destruction. Much of the blame was directed at radical, fundamentalist Islam, and people in the West began to ask what it was inside Islam, some spirit or some genie, that had somehow stopped it from reforming as other religions had done?

To my amazement, I discovered that Tunisia had already gone through an inner spiritual reform of Islam. The country began its reform, not only of Islam from within Islam, as early as the 1830s and, for most of that time, it had been moving along this path until the 1980s, when trouble erupted for reasons that were largely rooted outside the country. Tunisia's had been a successful and harmonious reform which had led directly to the healthy and progressive state of the nation by the 21st century. Yet few outside Tunisia knew of this story.

Late one Sunday afternoon during the spring of 2002, I drove out to La Marsa, one of those flower-filled seaside towns on the coast just outside Tunis, in order to delve deeper into this important stage of Tunisian history. I was going to meet one of the people who could best define the spirit of that special time. It took some searching, but finally my driver and I found Professor Mohamed El Aziz Ben Achour, a tall, spare, handsome man, a direct descendant of one of the most distinguished of the great Andalusian Moorish families. He

lived in a beautiful, weathered old mansion by the sea. The Ben
Achour house had very tall ceilings and perfectly understated, elegant
furnishings, with pictures of his forebears, many of them in military
uniform with medals worn proudly on their chests, and all with the
same spare visage and long, aquiline nose as he. I thought at first that
they were Turkish, but no, they were Moorish and had fled to Tunisia
in 1611. The reason we finally found the house was that it was on
Ben Achour Street!

'My family were intellectuals and magistrates, and the family have
been here since the 17th century,' the professor began, as we sat in
very straight chairs in a small circle. 'My family played a role in the
development of the university. And it is all the more interesting given
that the reformists were members of the *ulema* – they were
theologians themselves. My grandfather, Tahar Ben Achour, spared
no effort in reform. He played an important role in the reform of
education as dean of Zeitouna University in the 1930s.'

What did 'reform' mean at that time? I asked.

'For him, it meant unburdening the Muslim religion and getting rid
of everything that was not part and parcel of the original traditions,'
he answered. 'This was the result of a popular culture, but at the
same time it was also the result of underdevelopment. He was
advocating a return to the sources and to the true spirit of Islam – and
to my grandfather, the true spirit was faith. There was erudition, but
at the same time there was an openness to other religions and
cultures. He was a great theologian. In other words, he was versed in
Arabic language and Islam but he was also open to Western
civilisation.'

As the sun began to set over La Marsa, we sat drinking tea from
delicate little cups, and fruit juice from inscribed glasses. We fell
deeper into our discussion, and Professor Ben Achour explained the
history of the reformist movement. 'When the movement started
between the 1830s and the 1860s, it was undoubtedly a debate
between the defenders of reform and the conservatives,' he began.
'And what is most interesting is that, by the beginning of the 19th
century, the debate itself was taking place within the sphere of the
theologians themselves, between the modernists and the
traditionalists. The movement continued until the independence of

the country. Tunisian Islam played an important role in the reformist trend thoughout the entire Muslim world.'

And Why was That?

'Because Tunisia is a small country that has merit because of its founding texts,' he went on. Then he listed them for me, as a veritable shopping list of social progress reports. There was the book written in 1867 by the great Muslim reformer Khereddin al-Tunisi, *The Surest Path to Knowledge to Know the Condition of the States*. This was the first essay written in the Muslim world that called for the adoption of liberal political institutions inspired by the West. Not only was the writer not a theologian, but the Muslim clerics actually helped him write the book, illustrating the unusual depth and scope of the impulse for change in the society. The 1861 Constitution meanwhile, was the first constitution in the Arab world. Although in the beginning it existed only in a timorous way, its spirit remained so vivid that the largest party in Tunisia, the 'Destour', later renamed the 'Neo-Destour', and then the 'Constitutional Rally', was named after it. In 1930, in response to the need to emancipate women, came another important text, this one called *Our Women in Religion and Society*, by the reformist scholar Tahar Haddad.

But why Tunisia? I pressed him further. Why should this small country with so few apparent resources have started a sucessful process so long ago while even today, most Arab and Muslim countries are not even asking the relevant questions?

He sat back thoughtfully and pondered for a moment. 'You have to place it all in context,' he answered. 'You shouldn't forget Istanbul and the Ottoman empire. The reformist movement started earlier there, within the imperial government, when it was facing the threat of foreign powers. The reform movement within Islam appeared in Turkey, in Tunisia and in Egypt under the ruler Muhammad Ali after the Napoleonic invasion. In the Ottoman world, reform started with an awareness that the state was underdeveloped and was lagging behind the West. The Turks came here in the 16th century but the cultural personality of the country took over from them. Tunisia always tried to strike a balance between the local Arab heritage and foreign influence and we always tried to strike a balance in the social structure between tradition and modernity. It was all fragile in the beginning, of course...'

I left after two hours of talk, just as the moon was coming up over the little city. I had a distinct feeling of well-being. I was beginning to piece together more of the brightly coloured glass of this new part of the mosaic.

The Ottomans Come

The reform movement did indeed begin to speed up when the Turks became the newest conquerers of Tunisia. Their armies arrived in 1574, and Tunisia became part of the Byzantine and Ottoman Empire. Once again, the forms of the government changed. The Turks set up another government, 'The Regency', in which a Pasha was appointed as the far-away Sultan's representative. The Pasha in turn was supported by a military council or *divan* headed by a chief of staff first called a 'dey' and then a 'bey' who generally supervised everything. (Some of the Ottoman's nomenclature must have sounded comical, even to people who did not speak Turkish: a dey and a bey were not enough, they had to have a 'beylerbeg' ruling from Algiers!) The names of the beylical dynasties do not exactly trip off the tongues of foreigners, although many were brilliant and socially progressive rulers and dynasties: the Aghlabids, the Fatimids, the Zirides, the Almohads, the Hafsids and the Hussainids, to name some of the more notable ones.

Turkish rule was actually quite a loose and progressive regime, and the interior was largely left alone, known as a 'zone beyond control'. Much of the exquisite construction work in Tunisia was accomplished during the Ottoman period: the elaborately decorated palaces, the fine inlaid work, the system of *ribats* or fortresses along the coast, the stunning mosques and palaces. But the Ottomans were not only a great military and artistic empire, they also had a genuinely reformist streak which found fertile ground in Tunisia. There emerged at this time a new aristocracy, the families with a strong Turkish strain who were called *baldis*. They had a strong social conscience that paralleled their commercial talents. Part of the reason for this was that they wanted to rival Europe, so they supported the creation of efficient public services. In fact, Tunisian development under the beys was unique for an Arab land. Their political rule, which lasted until 1957, and is known as the 'beylical' period, also oversaw vast changes in the thinking of the élites and of the people.

Islamic reformism began first in Turkey and Egypt, but it reached its zenith in Tunisia, in great part as a response to the political, social and economic challenges of a far more advanced Europe. Thinkers such as the famous scholar and statesman Khereddin al-Tunisi, virtually unknown in the West even today, had been sold as a *mameluk* or slave-warrior from one of the military ruling families of Egypt to the Tunisian ruler Ahmed Bey and, typical of the progressive trajectories of the time, the bey, realising his talent, sent him to study at the Ecole Polytechnique in France in 1853.

Certain questions haunted these men. The Egyptian warriors had been defeated by Napoleon's army and, as it so often does, defeat sparked the need on the part of the vanquished to know how and why they had been so humiliated. Did they need to adapt some of the qualities, institutions and tactics of the conqueror? Did they need to change themselves completely? Many headed to Europe to find the answers to their questions for – if only to save their own souls – they had to find the reasons for the flaws in their society, without losing their own theologies and philosophies.

The young Khereddin studied hard and discovered that the European form of consultative government, known as *shura* in Islam, far from being anti-Muslim, was exactly the form of government enjoined by the Koran and the Hadiths. But Khereddin was not in favour of adapting French and other European ideas willy-nilly. His vision was to form a strong and just government which would be successful enough to command and to hold the loyalty of the people.

The respected Arab author Khaldun al-Husry, son of Sati al-Husry, one of the leading early proponents of secular Arab nationalism, wrote of this early process of Tunisian philosophical and theological give-and-take with other systems, 'Nowhere is this historical phenomenon of fighting a superior civilisation by adopting its own weapons, and the progression from borrowing the military and material elements of the culture to the appropriation of the non-military and non-material elements, illustrated as clearly as in the writing of Khereddin al-Tunisi.'

The prominent Anglo-Arab professor, Albert Hourani, based for many years at St. Antony's College, Oxford, pointed out in his later writings that the main ideas of the Enlightenment were not strange at all to Muslims. 'The idea that man fulfills himself as a member of society, that good society is based on a principle of justice and that the purpose of the government is to ensure the welfare of the ruled, is embedded in Islamic doctrine,' he wrote in 'Nineteenth Century Arab Thinkers and Revolutionary Ideas' from his book, *Arabic Thought in a Liberal Age*. What was new to Islam, 'was the idea that people could and should participate in the process of government, be educated for that opportunity and that laws can change according to circumstance.'

One example of the changes that were taking place in the country, is to be found in al-Husry's *Three Reformers: A Study in Modern Arab Political Thought*, in which he claims that dictionaries printed in Tunisia as late as 1867 retained the classical definition of *watan* as a place of birth, and did not mention *wataniyya*, which had been introduced into Tunisian thought to explain the concept of 'love of one's country'.

What was happening naturally in Tunisia was what other countries would struggle over in the 20th century. The individual Tunisian tribesperson was in the process of becoming a responsible Tunisian citizen of a coherent nation.

Another shining scholarly light of the time, Abd al-Rahman al-Kawakibi, wrote that the problem was not that Islam was incapable of democracy, for the true structures of government in Islam were 'democratic and representative'. Absolutist rule was a corruption of these principles and was actually established late in Islamic history. This argument, advanced often in Tunisian history and indeed in Turkish and Egyptian history too, attempted to prove that the original precepts of the Muslim faith had been set aside, or had been corrupted by popular culture and by under-development.

For the most part, the beys were responsible, practical, honest leaders. Their handsome, unsmiling faces are to be found today in the photographs displayed of them, with their tasteful uniforms, their chests modestly boasting small medals. They did not have that harsh, superior look of most authoritarian leaders and, in fact, most had marked streaks of progressive good governance. Ahmed Bey (1839-55), Muhammad Bey (1855-59) and Muhammad Sadiq Bey (1859-83) were all enlightened and intelligent men who travelled to Europe and, like their brothers in the Ottoman Empire, were scrutinising the Industrial Revolution for hints on how to order a modern Muslim state. In doing so, they reached out to citizens of differing backgrounds to rule the state, to Greeks, Circassians and Egyptians.

Under these men, the 'Fundamental Law' of 1857 was passed, assuring equal treatment, equal rights and opportunities of work for all persons living in the Regency – an astonishing development for the Middle Eastern world at this time. That 'Fundamental Law' was replaced in 1861 by the first Tunisian Constitution, already praised by Professor Ben Achour, which required each bey to swear allegiance to it, and to promise to serve and uphold the state. Such a document had never before been seen in the Middle East. It was during this age that Khereddin, when he became Prime Minister, took a giant step forward in education, when in 1875 he bypassed the old Zeitouna mosque university and opened the influential Sadiki College.

It is important to remember that these men were not questioning the values and principles of Islam, but were seeking to bring the scientific and technical aspects of Western education into Tunisian culture. They failed for the moment, largely because yet another invader was waiting at the gates. So it was that when the French came boldly as colonisers, they had only to place the institutional form over the political and spiritual forms that were already well embedded into the society. As Pierre Rossi points out in his writings on the Bourguiba period, 'It was no crude society that France was tackling in 1881 but on the contrary a kingdom where its influence was going to superimpose itself on a political and cultural structure already endowed with the legacies of five huge empires, those of Carthage, Rome, Byzantium, the Caliphs and the Turks.'

Prime Minister Khereddin, meanwhile, was fated to resign and lived out the rest of his life in Constantinople, where he became the Ottoman Sultans' Grand Vizier and tried once again, this time from the banks of the Bosporus, to reform the entire Ottoman empire.

The French Spirit

When the French occupied Tunisia in 1881, they used a tactic perfected by many peoples whom history had carried to a level of national overconfidence, putting them in 'imperial' mood. They used – and in fact, in part, created – a situation of threat towards the desired territory, then proceeded to exaggerate that threat and to act upon it. What they were really planning was to gain control of the entire rich, cultured region of the Maghreb from Morocco via Algeria to Tunisia. They used the threat of a group of Tunisian rebel tribesmen who were raiding France's Algerian territories and aiding anti-French rebels in the Aures Mountains. Most unfortunately, these rebels had a fondness for attacking foreign ships on the northern shores of the Maghreb, but then, this was hardly new. The United States had already become involved in a war in 1815 off the Barbary Coast of North Africa in what is today Algeria, where corsairs or pirates began attacking Americans and holding them as slaves, until the early American government sailed into Algiers and cleaned them out.

While it was capturing Tunis, France was also being troubled by the actions of the Italians, for during the 1860s they were again weaving illusions of reconstituting the Roman Empire, centred once more around Tunisia and Libya. By 1881, there were more Italians than French in Tunisia, 11,200 against 2,000; even today there are more Tunisians of Italian background than of French.

The French invaded Tunisia in order to control the Mediterranean. The Bey fled to Kairouan, where a hapless call for a *jihad* against the meddlesome infidels was raised unsuccessfully for a very short time, and peace was restored to Tunisia under the Treaty of Bardo on May 12, 1881. At that moment, France effectively began ruling Tunisia. The French Prime Minister went to the National Assembly in Paris and announced with notable immodesty, 'I have Tunisia in my pocket.'

In 1883, the Tunisian ruler Ali Bey was pressured into signing the Treaty of La Marsa, which gave France full authority over domestic as well as foreign affairs. And once again in its richly woven, but often difficult history, Tunisia was subjected to another entire change of authority, of structures and of systems.

Tunisia was now under a French Protectorate and ruled by Le Controle, under the French Resident-General who was the senior official. In theory he advised the Bey, but in practice the Bey advised him. The South, always different and difficult, was left under separate French occupation. In the cities, departments, or French *directions,* were organised as the structure of a modern state. Just as Arabic had taken over from the Punic language, so French took over from the Arabic in most public affairs. In foreign affairs, Tunisia was not permitted to conclude any treaties without the consent of France.

Politically, the old Turkish-imposed beylical system was dying, and a new age was dawning for Tunisia – but exactly what kind of age was it? The Tunisians would soon find out. The French Protectorate would, in practice, move the long road of Tunisian integration of peoples and classes into a still larger and more complex mosaic. They reformed the court system, consolidated all foreign debt, substituted a modern system of buying and selling, and profit and loss for the old tradition of barter. Railways were built and a proud electric suburban train, which is still valiantly running, revolutionised travel between Tunis, Carthage and La Marsa along the coast. The phosphate mines in the South were further developed. The French also dramatically reformed the system of land ownership. Surely great injustices were committed in the redistribution of the land in 1885, in the Land Registration Act, when all land titles were placed before a council, and European colonists flocked to Tunisia to claim this 'free' land; but at the same time, production on the land increased immeasurably, creating a truly modern and productive agricultural country. The new basis of power was no longer land but the produce taken from it, and the traditional alliance between 'palm tree, water and man' of the Tunisian author Muhammad Zarruq, was largely past. Many displaced Tunisians were thus unwillingly transformed into a working class.

The Tunisian man and woman had been freed from the tribal chief, and from the personal concern that family and tribal suzerainty often assured, and was now under an impersonal owner interested in him only as a cog in the production machine. Among the gains, much was lost. The village storyteller, who had captivated children with his great deeds of Islamic heroes, was replaced by the village school. Ironically, the new Tunisian independence leaders would, above all else, embrace the school as their way out of the Protectorate.

The French reign was, by and large, a peaceful one, although there were periods of substantial repression. But because it was predominantly peaceful, the Tunisians could focus on the Western ideas they wanted to accept – or were forced to accept – in order to modernise. Thus they were spared the endless, bloody civil wars and conflicts of neighbours like Algeria, Libya and the African countries to the south. In addition, for the first time, young Tunisians, who were now going to France to be educated, found Frenchmen and women who were not like the 'colons' or colonisers. By the time World War Two broke out, 60,000 Tunisians were serving in the armies of France. They came into contact with workers from all over Europe and learned about trade unions, higher wages and just working conditions.

Tunisia was now no longer a country of desert pathways, dirt roads and shadowy passageways winding among the craftsmen of the souqs. It was rapidly becoming a country of roads that were going somewhere. The oxen or donkeys carrying vegetables to the souqs would soon give way to cars and trucks carrying products to market. The Berbers began looking down from their mountain fastnesses with curiosity for the first time in their history and, with new confidence, thought that the valleys didn't look so bad after all. Tunisians were being uprooted from their traditional ways of life, but, unlike the situation for many others at their stage of development, they had a new and modern way of life open to them; they were planning now, and moving. It would not be long before they would be out there drawing white lines down the black paved highways.

Habib Bourguiba drew brilliantly upon all of these cultures, civilizations and historic experiences. He would need the wisdom of every one of them as he began his presidency.

3. From Bourguiba to Ben Ali: *From Father to Brother*

'It is intolerable that girl pupils should go in to school rigged out in a dishcloth.'

President Habib Bourguiba

The Appearance of Independence

When Habib Bourguiba became president of the new, independent Tunisian Republic in November 1957, the country already had much of the look of a developed country about it. The Francophone surface, the cultured and cultivated society, the refinement of its dreamy, ethereal coastal cities spreading out along the sea from the capital of Tunis, all proclaimed to the eager visitor that this was indeed already a 'different' kind of 'developing' country, particularly for the turbulent and unsettled Arab world. And in many ways – in great part due to the unique outlook and tactics of Bourguiba and his team of independence fighters – it was.

But underneath that engaging and reassuring veneer of gentility and movement, Tunisia was still a poor country. At the time of independence, the country's per capita income was only US$120, which was even then one of the lowest in the world (the figure included the incomes of the European section of the population as well as those of the Arab and Berber populations). Despite the changes in the education system in the 19th century, the masses still remained untutored – the literacy rate in the year of independence was an abysmal 28 percent. Within Islam, what the President called the 'old turbans,' or the traditional old-style Muslim men, still wielded substantial power to obstruct. Independence for the new country, with four million inhabitants and a 'homeland' of 50,000 square miles, 'took us by surprise', Bourguiba said in the beginning, as Tunisia immediately experienced a huge loss of capital and skills when more than half of the French residents left almost at once for France.

The seemingly endless wars next door in Algeria constantly threatened Tunisia with instability, while even at home internal disorder became the real 'order' of the day, as French police marauded the country at will, supporting the many settlers who refused to give up the estates awarded them by the Protectorate. Socially, too, the situation was ominous. Simple tribespeople, uprooted from their past lives in the countryside, poured into the expanding slums of Tunis, at least 350,000 of them unemployed and many quite simply hungry. Sociological and class differences were growing between the people of the South, who generally spoke only Arabic, and the urbane, French-speaking architects of independence. (The Southerners now often referred to them, in distance and in derision, as 'Those Men in Tunis'!). 'How, under such conditions, are we to assert Tunisian sovereignty and build the new state?' Bourguiba cried at one point. 'You might as well try to unravel a silk thread from a blackberry bush.'

And so, first, the new president took many actions that would underline and characterise everything that was to come and that would, in later years, illustrate how he had been able to make the important jump from independence fighter to effective leader. He initiated large public works programmes, he attended to the protection and restoration of the soil of the land and he absorbed much of the unemployment by paying subsistence level wages for work. These steps alone at least kept the country going. From the beginning, in part because such explorations challenged the intricacies of his mind, he also pored over the deeper questions. How could he integrate the society's nomads, who now risked losing their very identity as they were brought into a larger, less exclusive and more sedentary society and cut off from their family and tribal customs? He would inaugurate development programmes in their areas that respected their traditions. How could he make the 'new Tunisians' in politics represent not only their narrow tribal, family or even regional grouping, but the entire country? He inaugurated new laws by which the governors and all the deputies in the national assembly were required to represent the whole country, and not just one region or grouping, thus cutting them off from too great a dependence upon narrow regional issues and pressures. What was he to do with the thousands of poor, pitiful beggar children who were roaming hopelessly around the country after independence? Bourguiba formed dozens of 'children's villages', where they were housed, taught and prepared to become citizens of the 'new Tunisia' and where, most important of all, they were given the proud name of 'Children of Bourguiba'.

In a letter to his son during the independence struggle, when the boy was completing his own legal studies in Paris, Bourguiba summarised clearly what he saw as his intent and his mandate concerning the development of his people: 'It is the peculiar quality of condemned people,' he wrote. 'They want very much to be free, but they wait for liberation from a miracle from outside. This miracle will not come if they do nothing from within.' He was romantic about what could be, utterly and ruthlessly clear about what was. As late as 1962 in a speech in Tunis, Bourguiba was saying with an honesty and a clarity so rare in the Middle East of that day as to be unique, 'we must look reality in the face. Tunisia consists of separate social layers and does not yet enjoy that complete harmony which makes up the balance of a nation.' In fact, this had long been a constant in his thinking. At a 1937 party congress, he had said, 'There is no use hiding how far the Tunisian people are from being a mature people.'

The independence generation had constantly claimed to represent the 'will' of the Tunisian people, but its closely guarded secret was that there really was no definitive national will, and that they themselves had to plant it, create it and nurture it.

Bourguiba wanted development – it was the life-blood that ran in his veins – but he wanted it on distinctly different terms from virtually all the leaders of his generation. He would not watch his people driven to distraction by too rapid a pace of change, as had happened in so many countries which had tried to develop beyond a traditional man or woman's capacity to absorb and (a favourite Tunisian word) 'digest' that change. Eternally the maestro, he was forever instructing his people and urging them on, because he believed them capable of more than they had been, and of far more than they had done. Perhaps his break with traditional religion emerged from the fact that he never believed that anyone was destined or damned to eternal poverty or hopelessness. He talked of ideas not heard in the rest of the modern Middle East, such as creating within the spirit of his people, a 'psychological independence'. Thus, culturally above all, he began to put into place the elements that would truly lead the country to true independence.

One of the first apparent contradictions in this picture was the fact that Bourguiba was an authoritarian leader, reigning over such a consultative and yet clearly one-party state that they called him not only the 'Supreme Combatant' but also the 'Presidential Monarch'. And yet the entire thrust of his work was to force his people to think for themselves. How could it all fit together? Because Tunisia was an ongoing process, based on day-to-day and generation-to-generation development. What was appropriate for one day or one generation might not be appropriate for the next. In his book, *Party and People, A Study of Political Change in Tunisia*, the Swedish author Lars Rudebeck wrote of how, 'Bourguiba wanted to stress "psychological revolution," he wanted to create a climate of opinion that was favourable to modernisation through education, propaganda and structural reforms.' Moreover, Bourguiba believed that, 'until such a "revolutionary spirit" had at least begun to permeate the people, no radical reforms would be effective...'

To accomplish what he wanted without more interference from outside than he already had, Bourguiba explained at the very beginning that he had nothing against any system in the world, even international Marxist socialism or regional Arab nationalism (he did, but never mind). And in fact, for the first five years of the young country's life, his economic plans were imprinted with a socialist and collectivist spirit. But on a broader level, he would have no part in 'putting some foreign theory into action', because Tunisia would be guided 'solely by the criteria of reason'. His was to be the victory of disciplined and careful rationalism in a sea of careless and turbulent nationalism.

Yet at the same time, Bourguiba's image of himself could hardly be said to be modest. He saw himself as Prometheus; he had dared to steal the fire of heaven to act out the role of saviour; but he knew too that he had to create more than smoke from that eternal flame and that he had to create products and agricultural goods to feed the far more complicated demands of everyday life. Bourguiba looked out and he saw not eternal arguments about nationalism and pride, but the production line, the grape harvest, the consultative party meeting, the constantly evolving political process and the white line down the black road across the desert. Bourguiba did not dwell on what or who had brought the Tunisians down – he simply did not have time for that. Like his hero, the pivotal Turkish reformer Atatürk, he concentrated on acknowledging Tunisia's own mistakes and rectifying them. Even after he was president and he had built five glorious palaces for himself, and surely knew how to live the quintessentially good life, one of the amazing things about Bourguiba was that, until the very end – indeed, until the last, declining, potentially tragic years – he never really allowed his own admitted taste for grandeur to come at the expense of his people's welfare.

In the end, his 'victory' was never an exercise in orgiastic rhetoric but a series of small steps, none of which would appear to be inexorable, but which would, in time, become irreversible. Other nationalist leaders of his era saw victory in terms of a series of theatrical and rhetorical leaps designed to impose their generally anti-modern and anti-technical charisma over their people, even as they built roads that went nowhere.

The Third World Illusion
In addition to Marxism and other fixed ideologies in the Arab world such as the secular Syrian and Iraqi Ba'ath parties, Bourguiba was also up against 'Third Worldism'. There were the First and Second Worlds of Western democracy and Eastern Communism, and then

there was the 'Third World' of countries which had just emerged from painful and humiliating colonial eras in Asia, Africa, the Middle East and Latin America. They were overwhelmingly characterised by poverty, ignorance and a total lack of any of the characteristics that were basic to development.

In fact, 1956, the very same year that Bourguiba was readying himself to take power, marked the banner year of the Non-Aligned Movement of Third World Countries. Suddenly, in the wake of the anti-colonial struggles of the post-World War Two period and in the often delirious euphoria of the years that followed the end of the War, these countries would go the 'Third World Way'. Their voices were exorbitantly anti-colonial, super-nationalistic and pretentious. Their leaders would turn their backs not only on many parts of the West, but on anything to do with Westernisation that they felt was incompatible with their traditions. Thus they found emotional, if not economic, solace in non-aligned movements like the Organisation of African Unity, which believed that a declaration of independence, economic progress and political representation was infinitely more agreeable than the long and patient business of educating their people and preparing their cultures for change. Influenced by Marxist philosophy and by old tribal customs, these people most often saw economic development as simply using influence in international organisations to force the developed world to divide up its wealth with them, whether by shaming them or threatening them. Bourguiba had had men and women like this in his Neo-Destour party but, not surprisingly, he had successfully purged them along the way.

How emotionally gratifying was the 'play' on the extravagant political stage of the time. In the 1950s and '60s, men like Egypt's Gamal Abdel Nasser, China's Chou en-Lai, India's Jawaharlal Nehru, Indonesia's Ahmed Sukarno, Ghana's Kwame Nkrumah and Guinea's Ahmed Sekou Toure strode like giants across this new world, employing such superb theatrics that many confused their presumed confidence with the aplomb of hereditary monarchs, and their inordinate demands upon the First World as somehow moral. (After all, it was surely they, and not the unusual Bourguiba, who had the ear of the modern age). These leaders met in the spring of 1955 at Bandung in the interior of Java at a conference organised by

Indonesia, Burma, Sri Lanka, India and Pakistan, with 29 countries representing, as they stressed at the time, 'more than half the world's population!' At Bandung, which was to become the era's defining conference, the pushy, irrational but enormously confident Third World leaders would establish their new independence. They were highly vocal on the reluctance of the Western powers to consult them, and they were especially critical of France's colonial policies in northern Africa. It took a lot of talking, but the delegates did finally decide to condemn the Soviet Union for its 'colonial' policies, as well as the West, which made them more proud of their moral superiority than ever.

Then, in 1956, Nasser nationalised the Suez Canal, built by the British and the French in 1869, and when the two European powers attempted to retake it by force, the Americans successfully moved against them. That same year, Fidel Castro was holed up in the dense mountains of the Sierra Maestra in eastern Cuba, plotting to overthrow the American-supported Batista dictatorship and provide the world with its first serious example of the Marxist guerrilla movements that would haunt the hemisphere for the next three decades. Meanwhile in Hungary, Soviet tanks were moving against Hungarians desperate for freedom, sounding the first warning of the eventual disintegration of the Soviet Communist empire.

But while all the rhetoric and posturing against the West might have been emotionally satisfying, it was and would turn out to be distressingly empty of palpable reality, for virtually none of these leaders understood what Bourguiba instinctively understood, which was that certain values of the West, which were really values of modernisation, would need to be injected laterally into their new societies before they could begin to take part even minimally in the processes of exchange, production and social reconstruction of the modern world.

Almost immediately, most of the Third World responded in unfeigned shock to the figure that this quirky leader presented in their world of endless talk and righteous rage. The first unforgivable thing he did was to bypass – even to the point of disregarding – the other Arab leaders' ferocious hatred of the former colonialists. To Bourguiba, such techno-gyrations were simply a waste of time, given the things that he really wanted to accomplish. So instead of railing against the French, he calmly allowed them to keep a base at Bizerte until they were finally thrown out in 1963. Let the French pay for Tunisia's security! He welcomed French investment and turned the Tunisian education system ever more strongly towards the model of the French system. But above all else in the gathering Middle Eastern storm of that period, he dared to challenge the 'common wisdom' in the case of that most favoured of modern Arab causes, the Palestinians.

Contrary to what many of his critics thought, Bourguiba sympathised with the plight of the hundreds of thousands of homeless Palestinian Arabs who had been displaced by the formation of the Israeli state in 1948 and who then, backed up by the other Arab states, waged war after disastrous war to destroy Israel. But he was too much of a realist to believe that anything could be accomplished that way. Bourguiba never called for a final peace settlement with Israel, or even, for that matter, for the recognition of Israel; he only put forward the idea of a temporary peace to settle the refugee question and, as always with his intricate mindset, he knew that this step could later be superseded by others. Given the totalist phase that was rapidly taking over the rest of the Arab leadership, Bourguiba was soon looked upon as a heretic of post-colonialism.

When in 1965 he travelled through the Middle East, supposedly to improve relations with his fellow Arab presidents, it did not exactly help his relations with his 'brothers' when he lectured the other leaders. 'At the rate things have been going for the last 17 years', he said, 'the Arabs have not made an inch of headway.' In Jericho, he blamed the fate of the Palestinians on 'the leaders of most states who do not face their responsibilities'. Never a piker when speaking of his own country, he then said that the other Arabs 'should proceed by stages – like Tunisia'. He told the Palestinians: 'Take a Palestinian state!' They despised him for it at the time, yet later, in 1982 after the invasion of Lebanon by the Israelis and the Palestinian leadership's dispersal, they gladly went to Tunisia, which was the one country that would still have them and where they could be relatively safe.

Much later, when the elderly Bourguiba was told in 1993 about the handshake between President Bill Clinton, Israeli Prime Minister

Yitzhak Rabin and Palestinian leader Yasser Arafat on the White House lawn over the Oslo Accords, he said only one thing: 'It's too late for too little.'

Most of the other leaders of his time were always too late, always behind every historic curve, always wasting time responding to the rest of the world. Bourguiba was a man who kept track of time like a jockey at the races, and indeed seemed to have a veritable socio-political clock ticking away in his wary head. He was seldom 'late' in his actions or in his planning. His life, his thinking, his dedication and his principles were all geared towards pre-empting history and thus mastering it, never to be carried away by it and most likely be drowned. That French base at Bizerte that raised so many nationalistic hackles? Such criticisms merely represented the thinking of limited and lesser minds – he dismissed them with a Gallic shrug. An eternal fight over Israel, eating up all the energies and hopes of generation after generation? Take what you can get, consolidate and then move on; if you must get even, have the sense to do it from a position of strength and not weakness. What serious man could be bothered with losing because of unbridled ego or the extravagances of rhetoric when you could win real advantage?

President Bourguiba immediately put 30 percent of the budget into education, 30 percent into social programmes and the rest into government services. Thus, virtually alone in the Arab world, he began patiently laying the long-term basis for a modern state.

He was not, however, alone in history. In his own way, he was building upon the legacy not of the failed eras of Arab civilisation, but of the great ones. The Seljuks and Abbasids of Baghdad, the Moors of Spain, the Ottoman and Atatürk reformers of Turkey: those were his models and predecessors. In the back of his mind, he saw the days when the great Arab universities of Damascus and Baghdad saved classical civilisation for the entire world by protecting and preserving Greek manuscripts and history, when Greece was being overrun by savages. His administration was going to modernise Tunisians, their bodies and more importantly, their minds, and bring both into accordance with a new culture that would be a legitimate – and legitimising – mosaic of all the early Tunisians, alongside the best of the West.

Forming the New Tunisian Man and Woman

It was on my second trip to Tunisia in 1997 that I began to understand fully what Bourguiba had been doing. I went to see the prominent educator, family specialist and Minister of Education, Hatem Ben Othman. His career had been made by university education and his essential modernity was illustrated by the fact that he had been a past president of the volunteerist Kiwanis Clubs' social programmes related to education. He greeted me in his office which was, like so many of the other ministers' offices, set in a beautiful old building on the edge of the medina. He quickly launched into a description of the Tunisians' ideas about wealth and about Tunisia's reform -- really, a revolution -- in education.

'Tunisia is among the countries that are not wealthy in terms of oil and other primary sources of wealth,' he began, 'so in our history we have always paid attention to education and human resources. Since independence, education has been compulsory and enrolment is 100 percent. All of the books are subsidised. All households are aware that educating their children is a 'social promise' that they make to society, and this most definitely includes girls. Tunisians used to think that the best thing for a girl was to make a good marriage. Now, it is to get a good education. The law says education for boys and girls is compulsory, and families who do not send their children can be punished. Yet, the reasons for not sending children to school are decreasing, and many families don't want to keep girls at home any more because of economic reasons.'

How does he prepare Tunisian children to understand the past, the present and the future?

'Our entire objective is to find an equilibrium between our history, our communities and our groups,' he answered. 'We are Arab, African, Muslim, Mediterranean, Jewish. All of these groups shape what we call Tunisia today. The Tunisian who is looking forward to the future must have at least one foreign language. The children start with French in elementary school, with English from the eighth grade. There are six years of English, ten years of French. The law says that in the basic school, all courses are in Arabic. In the high schools, however, science, economics and technical subjects are given in French. Readings in business and computer sciences are in English.

We prepare the Tunisian of the 21st century by giving him or her the broadest education possible.'

And what about history?

'Previously, only Islamic and Arabic history was taught,' he went on. 'Now we realise that we have a very rich history that began 3,000 years ago. Until recently, for example, people forgot that Saint Augustine was Tunisian. In his age, all of Tunisia was Christian.' He paused, then began again with the qualifier that one hears over and over again in Tunisia. 'Don't forget what happened in Algeria,' he warned. 'We could have had that here. Before 1987, our teachers were preparing the children in fundamentalist ways. Today, there is no more risk of that. Today, everything is now tolerant, open, free. Students today will be very aware of being Tunisian, but will also be prepared for the outside world. We teach Islamic courses, but we emphasise the aspects of Islam that are for tolerance and that recognise other religions, as in Spain under the Moors. We are open to learning about all religions and theologies: Hebrew, Greek, Latin, English. Remember, the original Zeitouna mosque and university was 1,400 years old, one of the oldest in the world.'

And so, after I had said my *au revoirs* that day, I wandered over to see Zeitouna for the first time. To get to the mosque, you have to leave the Avenue Bourguiba, with its central walkway lined with trees and its elegant French mansions. Suddenly you are in the medina, a world of sensuous impressions, where the reflection of a sunbeam off a silver-hammered Tunisian mirror, or the lovely odour of a *narghile* or waterpipe suddenly assaults and awakens your feelings. You stroll down darkened alleyways, men hawking every sort of gold or silver treasure, when you happen upon an exquisitely painted and beautifully tiled old building with the bold black and white striped door decorations of the Moors. Then you turn a corner, and come face to face with the Zeitouna or 'Olive Tree' mosque.

It is still there today, this famous mosque built in 734 AD by the Umayyad Arabs. On the street side, its face is grey and a little forbidding, but when you walk up a flank of stairs and gaze into the centre of the old building, you find that the mosque itself is all grey and mellow, with a large central courtyard surrounded by 200 columns, all carried from the ruins of the city of Carthage after it was destroyed. I stood for a long time that day, looking into the central courtyard and thinking. I knew that it was here that the *ulemas* or priests themselves began to rally for reformation, to reinterpret Islam and to weed out what they saw as the corruption of religion through folk-cultural additions over the centuries. I knew, too, that it had been closed as a school in 1960 and replaced with an Islamic faculty that was part of the government-regulated University of Tunis. Today the mosque is purely a place of worship. University studies as well as regular religious education have been given over to state universities and to the burgeoning number of private universities.

I remembered the night I had gone to see the elegant Professor Ben Achour in his exquisite home in La Marsa on Ben Achour street, whose family had fled Catholic Spain in 1611 and had left such a brilliant mark on Tunisian education, thought and artistry. 'Remember,' he had said that night, 'Tunisia opted for a different approach from the rest of the Arab world, and integrated religion into the university and outside the mosque.'

In order to deal with education, Bourguiba first had to deal with Islam, particularly since he was continuing – now at full force – with the separation of education from the rote Islam that had been the norm. Here, once again, Bourguiba shocked the world. He was not only a sceptic, he was a Muslim who sought a rational interpretation of Islam. On the other hand, he was stunningly frank about deriding, even hating the retrogressive parts of Islam. Probably his intense sense of destiny had little to do with any religion – it might have diverted attention from himself and from his own sacred intentions.

His first attack was on the holy month of Ramadan, which is based on the lunar calendar and rotates around the year. It is one of the five pillars of Islam, during which Muslims fast all day and gather at night to eat and drink. To underline his strong feelings, and because of his polished sense of theatrics, he once posed slowly and dramatically drinking a glass of orange juice during Ramadan. As with so many aspects of Bourguiba's convictions, a good part of his objection to it was economic. He urged people to eat during the Ramadan fast because of health reasons, and because fasting interrupted economic activity. To make his views more palatable, he would argue that, since the struggle against underdevelopment was a form of 'holy war', the Prophet would surely allow the people to eat in order to fight this special *jihad* more thoroughly and successfully.

He lost the immediate Ramadan fight at the time, but he won the infinitely more important fight of separating Islam from education. This placed Tunisian Islam light years ahead of the rest of the Muslim world, and without question allowed it to avoid the terrible wars of religious fundamentalism that dominated the 1990s and the first years of the 21st century.

A Question of Women

There was no single question in Tunisia, nor indeed anywhere in the Middle East, that was as central and as profound to every aspect of development as the question of women, and Habib Bourguiba was, from the very beginning, amazingly sensitive to it. He took on what are probably the most contentious aspects of traditional Islam, the issues of polygamy and the veil.

In later years one of the ministers told me how, in the typical Tunisian way, they decided to dismantle the practice of taking four wives. Determined to ban polygamy, they searched the Koran and soon discovered that, in order to take more than one wife, a Muslim man must treat all equally. 'We started on it a year and a half after independence,' he said, 'and we found that, based on the verse in the Koran, a man needed to be fair to all four wives. Yet the Almighty said you can't be fair to all four.' A small smile of triumph played upon his lips. 'And so we could outlaw it.'

Bourguiba was also ruthless on the question of the wearing of the veil. He seemed to be almost enraged by it, as though it were a personal affront. In by far the most famous words that he voiced on the subject, he said that girls should not go to school 'rigged out in a dishcloth.' Another time, he called it 'nothing but a sinister shroud that hides the face.' When he spotted a woman in the countryside he declared in his peremptory manner: 'That woman over there, let her take her veil off – she'll see better…' Marriage to a man her family chose for her? 'It is incomprehensible that a young girl should be forced to found a family with a man she does not love,' he proclaimed. 'The only thing that counts is the happiness of the young girl. Let the decision be left, then, to those whom the marriage concerns, the husband and the wife.'

Soon women simply began to drop the veil and to look openly around their world. It became a common sight to see a mother, still veiled and covered, walking with her fresh-faced daughter in her school uniform to school or to the medina. Once again in Tunisia, the generations had learned how to bridge differences without drowning in the rivers of change.

From the very beginning of the republic, all of these precepts were incorporated into the 1956 *Code du Statut Personnel* or 'Code of Personal Status', which effectively placed just about every principle that women needed for equality, justice and dignity directly before the people. The code forbade polygamy, introduced judicial divorce for women as well as men, set a minimum age for marriage and gave women the right to vote and run for political office. Education was made free and compulsory for both sexes. But perhaps most importantly, the assumptions of Tunisians about male-female relations began to change once those assumptions had been contradicted by the laws of independence. A woman's work, for example, was no longer held to have a negative effect on her family life. On the contrary, it was assumed that it would help her family as well as helping her. 'By her labour, a woman or young girl assures her existence and becomes conscious of her dignity,' Bourguiba said in a speech in 1962.

So it was that on another afternoon during my time in Tunisia, in order to gain more of an understanding of the philosophical basis of this crucially important reform, I went back to the medina, to another glorious old palace, in order to talk to the Minister of Women's Affairs, Naziha Zarrouk. She was a robust and intelligent woman who, like most Tunisian women, had ideas about feminine equality that were often quite different to those of many feminists in the West.

'It is a question of mutual responsibility,' she began, speaking of the changes for women that were still virtually unheard of in most of the rest of the Arab world. 'We came to install a new state of mind, not only in terms of equality but in real partnership. Everything would be based upon mutual responsibility and in working hand in hand. Family... business... scholarship... divorce... After our laws and amendments, for instance, the wife can even be the "head of the

family". Another important trend is the creation of a fund for
divorcees, in case the father does not pay his support. Women can
give their nationality to a child from a non-Tunisian husband with
the consent of the husband if they live outside the country. We
enforce equality of salary, and in cases of violence against a wife, the
penalty is increased over other cases.'

Mrs. Zarrouk went on to become the country's ambassador to
Lebanon in 2002, the first Arab woman ambassador to be posted in
another Arab country. This is typical of the way in which capable
people can advance in Tunisia.

Philosophically, the Tunisian way of looking at women was a
mixture of practicality, cultural disgust about injustice and the idea that
both men and women were responsible for the development of their
country. As Mrs. Leila Ben Ali, the wife of the second president of
Tunisia, succinctly put it in one of her speeches on women's rights,
'Political involvement is a patriotic duty which every member of society
is called upon to discharge within freedom, equality, democracy and a
sense of duty.' In short, women's rights are not only there for women's
own enjoyment and equality, but to enable them to contribute to the
broader society. This principle is expressed in Chapter Six of the
Constitution, which provides that all Tunisians are entitled to the same
rights, are equal before the law and have the same obligations.

Why did women's emancipation go so far in Tunisia, especially
compared with virtually all of its neighbours? There was, of course,
the tradition of the ancient queens, reinforced by the fact that over
the centuries so many cultures played out their dramas in Tunisia,
giving the country the historic shape and mentality of an eternal
crossroads. But more importantly, from the 19th century onwards,
there were always several simultaneous internal revolutions going on
in Tunisia – in education, within Islam, in culture, in political
structures and in economic processes. In fact, the debate about
women's rights began as early as the 18th century, even in Islamic
thinking. It would have been odd, given this ferment, if women had
not reached out during this period of transition.

There is also the fact that, because of the essentially one-party state
that Bourguiba installed, which was natural to historic Tunisian
development, he and his party could authorise and enforce such an

initially unpopular edict as women's liberation. Without that authority at the centre that so many European Leftist thinkers deride in Tunisia, these reforms, which are essential to the entire makeup of the state, could never have taken place. Ironically, this central authority would turn out to be not so much coercive as liberating.

A Special Form of Governance
A polished Tunisian diplomat, Ambassador Noureddine Mejdoub, with whom I had a number of pleasant and provocative conversations both at his embassy and over lunch in Washington in the 1990s, once wrote me a cherished letter in which he addressed the differences between the American way of viewing, and criticising, our president, and the Tunisian Way. This happened to come during the troubling end of the Clinton administration. His letter emerged from one of our conversations about America at that traumatic time. 'On the shores of the Mediterranean,' he wrote, 'we have an instinctive respect for the Chief of State, all the more so when he succeeds in his mission of securing the public welfare. For the peoples of the Mediterranean, "Rex" means the one who guides and leads, while for the Anglo-Saxons, King or "Koenig" designates the strongest and the most powerful. This conflict is not one of vocabulary only. Our peoples do not expect to be governed by a mighty god but by men who have the right to make mistakes.'

This idea of governance does indeed run through much of the Arab world, and must be taken into consideration when studying the Tunisian model and attempting to impose it elsewhere. In Arabic, for instance, 'to govern' means essentially 'to judge' between people. And so the 'ruler' is a 'person appointed to judge among people'. Exemplifying the very best of this style of governance, the great Imam Ali bin abi Taleb, who was the son-in-law and cousin of the Prophet Mohammed and the first Imam of the Shiites, advised leaders, saying that, 'your concern with developing the land should be greater than your concern with collecting taxes, for the latter can only be obtained by developing; whereas he who seeks revenue without development destroys the country and the people.' How very Tunisian!

Following the spirit of such injunctures, Bourguiba and his party – which changed from the Neo-Destour to the *Parti Socialiste Destourien* or Destourian Socialist Party in 1964 and then to the *Rassemblement Constitutionnel Democratique* or Democratic Constitutional Rally Party of Bourguiba's successor in 1987 – never pretended that they represented any form of Western multi-party democracy nor, at this period in their national life, did they aim at being so.

This is the way it worked on a purely physical and structural basis: in 1956, Bourguiba divided the country into 14 areas or governorates (today there are 24), designated by the names of the capitals of the regions. These are split into delegations. The governors are more than bureaucratic officials – they could almost be considered the ambassadors of the head of state to the region. In the Tunisian way, power emerged from below and worked its way upwards through consultations at every level, until right at the top, the President made the final confirming decisions. It was something like the way the Communist parties might have worked, had they worked. Under Bourguiba, Tunisia was a one-party state, with the legislators called for six months to put their imprint on the party's thinking. All year round, ideas and observations bubbled up from the bottom of the party to the top.

This did not stop the early Tunisian leadership from making some substantial errors. Potentially the most dangerous ones were in the areas of land and the economy. But there was also the stunning fact, particularly in contrast to elsewhere in the Arab world, that Bourguiba and his leadership could change their minds.

Despite Bourguiba's dislike for philosophical Marxism and Third World economic posturing, modern Tunisia did not start out as a capitalist, free-enterprise nation, any more than it started out as a perfect democracy or a functioning civil state. In fact, the first years of the Tunisian experiment were actually socialist and collectivist, and this only led to economic turmoil. Bourguiba's economy minister Ahmed Ben Salah, author of the socialisation of the land, was given close to 900,000 acres of formerly French-held land, which he immediately turned into Yugoslav-style 'cooperatives'. As the French-language monthly, *Le Nouvel Afrique Asie*, wrote at the time, these experiments failed, as they did almost everywhere they were tried, 'because of the excess of heavy-handed and paralysing bureaucracy, which left no room for manoeuvre for peasants it claimed to modernise.' Since 70 to 75 percent of Tunisians still lived off the land, this was obviously a serious situation.

The Bourguiba government was also taking over the already weak economic structure in those years, an act that discouraged many in the small but dynamic Jewish community of between 2,000 and 3,000 people, mainly merchants and professionals. It was in those years that most of them left because of the sinking economy, although some also left because of the Israeli-Arab conflict. Finally, Bourguiba himself realised that even a Tunisian brand of socialism would not work, and he reversed the trend. Thereafter, in a series of complicated but effective laws, Tunisia aimed directly at creating a new class of 'proprietors' on the land that it had nationalised in 1964.

The Tunisians insisted that they had learned from the experience. Some even went so far as to say that they had learned they must be 'vaccinated' against both wasteful land programmes and against the later spectre of Islamic fundamentalism. 'We had two vaccinations in our society,' one of the leading ministers told me many years later. 'In the early '60s, the first was against the socialist land reform. Ben Salah introduced the Yugoslav system, with co-ops across the country which never worked. In four years we had bankruptcy. We changed and we were alert enough to stop the experiment. The second vaccination was in the 1980s against fundamentalism. When that became violent, the fundamentalists were throwing acid at women... they were slashing people with razor blades... they were setting off bombs on our streets... But we put the brakes on very urgently, and the opposition parties rallied around us. But we didn't do any of it with bullets. We were not going to give them martyrs.' He paused here and seemed to be thinking back to those years, thinking with sadness and with pride. 'You see,' he summed up, 'we had a vision of an Arab and Muslim country putting its house in order.'

The Troubled Eighties
By the mid-1960s and early '70s, after its ideological uprooting from the Tunisian style of socialism, Tunisia was already being recognised in the world as an experiment that 'worked' – or, at least, was

beginning to work. But once again, the Tunisian process of modernisation was momentarily stopped when one crucial element in the dynamic equation of evolutionary change upset the careful balance.

By the 1980s Bourguiba was getting old. The world around him had changed from the clear struggle of fighting the French to fighting spiritually corrosive new movements of absolutist ideas across the globe, and the 'Tunisian experiment' was in trouble. Around Tunisia, the original Third Worldism that Bourguiba had so scorned had given way to another new radicalism, within Islam itself. As early as the 1960s, new-style Islamic 'scholars', violent in their capacity and determined to create pure Islamist states in which they would govern and decide what faith was legitimate, began to appear in the medinas, in the mosques and in the institutions of Tunisia, as well as in the other major cities of the Muslim world. These were led by young Islamic 'preachers', often in mosques that sprang up of themselves, and they often had little to do with the traditional centres of Islamic thought like Cairo's authoritative Al Azhar university and mosque.

The true year of apocalyptic change across the whole region was 1979. The Soviets invaded Afghanistan that year, providing the impetus for the formation of an entire generation of Arab 'Afghanis' who were the precursors of Al Qaeda and other Islamist movements across the world. That same year, Ayatollah Khomeini took over in Iran, providing the first example of a 'pure' Islamist theological state and a pure example of Islamist repression. Within months, Islamist Iran was locked into a brutal war with secular Iraq, the first major confrontation of two opposing ideologies. In the First and Second worlds, Soviet Communism was beginning to fail, and certainly to fade as an example for the Third World. It would take another ten years for it to implode, but by the end of the '70s, it was clear that liberal democracy was winning the ideological battle for development. It was a world in ferment.

Despite Tunisia's modernisation – and in many ways, because of it – it would have been unusual for Tunisia to have been exempted, and it was not. The modern Arab world was in sobering decline. It had not been able to deal with its history or its humiliation. Governments were largely tyrannies or, at best, authoritarian governments with no checks and balances. They were falling not only behind the West but also far behind the new little states of Asia. Worst of all, the Arabs kept demanding, in distinctly anti-Bourguiba thinking: 'Who did this to us?' It could be the British and French, or the Israelis or the Americans, but it was seldom they themselves. Neurotic conspiracy theories abounded. 'How to put it right?' was instead the question that Tunisia, and Turkey and later Oman and Bahrain, were grappling with.

But the 'antibodies' that Ben Yahia had spoken of were no longer containing the diseases. In 1984 Tunisia erupted. In the midst of a drought that had damaged the crops, the price of bread rose 115 percent overnight, and troops had to be sent in to quiet the rioters. Over a hundred were killed before order was temporarily restored. The economy was once again stagnating, for Bourguiba was still embracing too rigid a model of statism and not giving business and commerce enough air. Tunisia was beginning to see what would become the scourge of the '90s; they were educating young Muslims without providing them with jobs, thus thwarting their energy and turning it towards radicalism.

These problems could have been contained had Bourguiba himself not been growing senile and slipping into incoherence. At his insistence he had been proclaimed President-for-life in 1974, and the Supreme Combatant was now focusing almost exclusively on himself. In place of the man of ideas and of his treasured rationalism, he now became a man of whims and tempers, a figure of dangerous potential tragedy. He would put a minister in one day, take him out the next; appoint two rival men for the same position, then accuse them of trickery. He divorced his second wife, having long before divorced his French wife, and accused her of 'contradicting' him. When he was told of the 1973 war between the Arabs and the Israelis, he only muttered, 'strawberries'. In 1974, he announced an astonishing 'union' with Libya, Tunisia's primitive desert neighbour, whose leader Muammar Khadafy was the very spirit and soul of foolish and destructive radicalism, and signed it on hotel stationery. This hapless, but revealing, manoevure was soon simply forgotten. When the Tunisian President visited Ronald Reagan in the White House in 1985, he interrupted the American President several times in order to enquire in French about issues he thought the man had neglected to mention; and at the State Department, he suddenly spoke personally to his female interpreter in French, saying that, 'if you were only 15 years older and I were 15 years younger, things might happen with us.' Participants in the meeting who understood French were horrified, while the interpreter blushed a number of shades of red.

These developments, in turn, gave both solace and an opening to the new Islamic movements, which from the 1970s onwards had paralleled the radical attraction and the societal threat of the ever-present Communists. They had also – and this would only really be understood later – adopted the Marxists' organisational tactics. First the Islamists moved in on the universities. These were always the pivot for revolution, because it was in these élite corrridors of learning that abstruse ideologies and philosophies could thrive, untethered from the practical needs of real, everyday people. Then they infiltrated the institutions of government, the police and also, to some extent, the army.

What is less known is the fact that one could already see the forms of the coming age in the Middle East in these Tunisian Islamists. They were closely related in spirit and even in tactics, for instance, to some of the earlier liberation movements, and they were also, on many levels, modern men. Just as in later years Israeli officials would be amazed at the technological knowledge of many of the radical Palestinian Islamists, and America would be astounded after 9/11 by the unexpected technical mastery of the Al Qaeda terrorists, many of whom had been educated in Western technology, so the Tunisian officials were when they discovered that the fundamentalists had huge technical and electronic arsenals. As Abdelbaki Hermassi wrote in his book, *The Islamist Dilemma*, this new period saw the emergence of new leaders 'that included professionals, manipulators of the masses, communications specialists, masters in swaying public opinion and experts in logistics. This generation of organisers, engineers and professionals was seizing the leadership from the established orators and cultural exponents.' But at the same time, the Tunisian Islamists, first in the *Mouvement de la Tendance Islamique* (MTI) or Movement of the Islamic Tendency and later under other names like *An Nahda* or The Renaissance Party, were forming. Their leaders travelled to Sudan to learn how to infiltrate state agencies and institutions and to Iran to see how to 'Islamise the streets'. They made avid students.

Few noticed in this era that, while all of these threatening changes were occurring on the surface of Tunisian society, other changes were taking place within the regime. It was in 1984, the year of the bread riots, that an attractive young general staff officer and intelligence man, with a record of accomplishment but as yet unknown to many Tunisians because of the secrecy of much of his work, had been called to head the National Security Department. Soon Zine el Abidine Ben Ali was appointed Secretary of State for National Security and then Minister of National Security and Minister of the Interior, and finally, in 1987, Prime Minister. Many observers just shook their heads and muttered: 'The classic man of the intelligence!'

Meanwhile, Bourguiba's moderation was being challenged frontally and dangerously. There had always been a radical streak inside the seemingly benign, rational Tunisian society, but until the '80s, it had been channelled into the fight against the French and the struggle for reform, all the while buoyed by the promise of the first presidency. Now those natural levels of moderation within society were being sorely tested because, as Abdelbaki Hermassi explained, 'The Islamicist movement thrived on the ideological looseness of the post-Independence state and has the capacity to attract many of those left behind by economic growth, or – to talk like the great German sociologist Max Weber – the proletarian intelligentsia who despair of the nationalist and socialist discourse.'

At first, the radical fundamentalist Islamist movement in Tunisia, as elsewhere, had only been active in the mosques and in theological circles, focusing on deviations and doctrinal questions much like those long faced by that mother of all the fundamentalist movements, the Muslim Brotherhood of Egypt. But now the small budding movements became ever more powerfully politicised under their leader, Rached Ghannouchi, a professor of philosophy with a charismatic rhetorical manner. He was destined to sit out the rest of his life in restless and accusatory exile in London, but not before he had seriously threatened the very existence of the entire modern Tunisian state.

Some try to explain the young man's transformation to Islamic radical by focusing on the status and place of his birth. He was born in 1942 in a small oasis, Al-Hama in the South, close to the Libyan border, one of the poorest and most remote areas in Tunisia. He had been forced to leave primary school for two years because of the poverty of his family. Historians sometimes call him the 'result of the Zeitouna system', by which they meant that he was deeply influenced by the old system of Islamic rote learning of the Koran. But just as the early great explorers like Marco Polo and Ibn Battuta had roamed the world simply looking for places and people, young men like Ghannouchi were now roaming the world looking for solutions to feelings of personal and national humiliation, and answers to questions of national development.

His was not a simple journey; he went to Syria, to Egypt and to Iran, but he also went to Europe. Typical of the odd voyages occurring among young Muslims of his time, he became fascinated by Albania, the most repressive Communist regime in the world, an 'attraction' that surely exemplified a certain originality. His epiphany apparently occurred while he was listening to Radio Albania in Cairo, and he later travelled to that strange country, with unknown results. After the Arabs' defeat of 1967 at the hands of the Israelis, Ghannouchi came to feel utterly despondent and hopeless. He let his beard grow – 'like Castro', he said – and then soon went over to the most radical Islamist line, complete with the issuing of theological *fatwas* or rulings giving him sacred permission to overthrow the Tunisian government. Meanwhile, the fundamentalist An Nahda set up a super-secret 'Special Apparatus' of intelligence and assassination within the already secret Islamist organisations which would carry out the coups and killings of heretics. They and they alone knew how to 'impose the will of the people!'

But it must also be seen, as a few perceptive writers have pointed out, that these Islamist groups across the Middle East, but particularly in the rather special case of Tunisia, were heartily influenced by the liberation movements, Marxist and otherwise, which had come before them in the Third World. Like Bourguiba and the Neo-Destour, the Islamists were struggling for a workable form of decolonialisation and for the construction of a modern nation-state. But the Tunisian Islamists saw Bourguibism as too culturally close to the West, as too much assimilated by it.

For a while, Ghannouchi and his followers seemed to accept the rules of the game – taking part in parliament, running for office and obeying the tenets of common civic action. But in truth, as would become obvious later, they were preparing for the final confrontation. In the end, their 'political' episode turned out to be another classic attempt by a radical group to appear to be what it was not in order to gain total power. To a substantial degree, the principles and tactics that would assault the West – the terrorist attacks in Europe throughout the '80s and '90s and, finally those in New York and Washington in 2001 – were tried but luckily never took root in this small and seemingly peaceful, progressive country.

At the same time, Bourguiba was making a series of potentially deadly mistakes regarding the Islamists. In the opinion of certain elements of his society, Bourguiba had pushed modernism-at-any-cost too fast and had woefully underestimated the powerful attraction of such (to him) despised retrogessive religious agents, thinking that the President-for-Life could always control events in the end with a wave of his polished hand. In fact, at one point the President had even encouraged the Islamists in the universities as a counterpoint to the Far Left and the Marxists.

In the single most comprehensive and fair-minded journalistic account of the time, entitled, 'How the Islamists Have Been Defeated', the prestigious French magazine, *Jeune Afrique*, no friend of the Right, wrote in the spring of 1999: 'To combat the strong General Union of Tunisian Students, headed by leftist elements, the government allowed the first Islamist militants to make their entry into the university. It even allowed them to build the first mosque in the university campus of Tunis, just next to the buildings of the National Institute of Engineers, which quickly became one of their strongholds... Having attracted in its wake many young men graduated from scientific universities, and having gained precious support from the middle class and the professional circles, the movement became an anti-authority catalyst.'

Now the confrontation between government and movements became deadly serious. Some extremists would be put in jail for their demonstrations, and for an armed uprising in 1980 in Gafsa, south-west Tunisia by a Tunisian commando group infiltrated from Libya and Algeria. From jail they watched the political takeover in Iran and nourished similar apocalyptic dreams for themselves. As the Bourguiba regime seriously faltered, due both to his increasingly strict controls over opposition parties and independent trade unions and his failing mental health, the Islamists succeeded in infiltrating the police and the army, where they went on recruiting binges for the 'final battle'. The government responded in 1986 by launching a new wave of arrests among the leaders of the Movement. Four were brought before the court and sentenced to death and three were executed for treason.

Still, it was far from over. On the night of August 2, 1987, four bombs exploded simultaneously in four hotels in Sousse and Monastir. These were masterful targets, in that they directly attacked the thriving tourism sector and, if continued, would surely turn away all foreigners and once again isolate Tunisia from the world. An official total of 12,700 Islamist militants were arrested, tried and sentenced to up to eight years in prison throughout the country between March and the end of August 1987. Police raids, house searches and torture were the order of the day, yet the Islamists were still able to organise 70 to 80 political demonstrations during this time. The government had acted firmly and often brutally, yet the dangerous situation was far from over. The central problem still remained; Habib Bourguiba was simply no longer capable of ruling and there was no assurance whatsoever that the radical Islamists, whose finale was a fascist Islam, would not still win. What was to be done?

The Decision of 1987

Tensions were building up at a murderous and unsustainable rate for Tunisian society. Bourguiba had summoned the then Prime Minister and Minister of the Interior Ben Ali on November 5. The President had become obsessed with a treason trial of Ghannouchi and wanted to put the man to death, much to Ben Ali's horror. But the Islamist coup to overthrow the government was planned for the night of November 8, 1987. A religious *fatwa* had been issued by sympathetic Islamic clerics to give sacred 'permission' to the Islamists. The

Islamists' 'Special Apparatus', or most secret parallel structure tasked with intelligence security and the orchestration of violence, was swinging into action. The former Minister of Justice Sadok Chaabane says that, 'At that time, the prisons were almost without walls; they had become permeable. From their cells, the movement leaders... gave their instructions and directed the operation.' The movement 'had at its disposal an élite troop experienced in martial arts and acts of terrorism. It had been trained in Iran and Afghanistan... Tens of thousands of grassroots militants were ready to trigger, throughout the country, more-or-less violent demonstrations aimed at bringing about the fall of the regime...' They would begin by taking Carthage Palace. It was a more dangerous time than many Tunisians realised at the time.

And then, very suddenly, it was over.

Many had regarded the sober, organised, handsome Zine El Abidine Ben Ali as merely a figure of the intelligence, as a man of force, and as a man who could only act ruthlessly against the Islamists but who could do little else. Most of these analysts were wrong.

As the Minister of the Interior, watching the state fall apart under the incoherent leadership of President Bourguiba and facing an Islamist coup as well as an attack on himself from some of Bourguiba's scheming courtiers, Ben Ali knew that he had to act – and he did.

At 5:30 a.m. on November 7, 1987, a grey and chilly autumn day, he telephoned the President to say that the time had come for him to retire and go home to Monastir and that, within an hour, he was going to announce his retirement on the radio. Ben Ali had obtained legitimate doctor's orders saying that the founder of the country, President Bourguiba, was no longer capable of ruling the country, an exigency that had been provided for under Article 57 of the Tunisian Constitution. Bourguiba first protested, but finally reportedly muttered in words typical of his mental state by then, 'You are right, I should have thought of it before.' He was then taken to his home in Monastir, back to the beautiful little white and blue city on the southern coast, where he would live out the rest of his days in peace and quiet, still respected and even revered, although now more warily so, until his death 13 years later.

Newly-named President Ben Ali visited him there every year, a tribute that was deeply Tunisian and which immensely pleased the average Tunisian, to whom such care and solicitude was merely an extension of their native sense of courtesy and balance.

In the end, Bourguiba had outgrown his early self, refusing to leave his position and become a wise counsellor during all those years when he could so easily have done so. He had been able brilliantly to seize power and to cement independence during its first and most difficult years, but he had not, in the words of the great sociological student of charisma, Max Weber, managed to 'routinise his charisma'. He had bravely travelled the impossible road from dedicated resistance fighter to traditional patriot, but in the end he had not been able to deal with the complex mature questions of a developing country. He had only been half able to lay the base for a true and deep institutionalisation of his society and, despite his impassioned desire to educate his people, in the end he had not given them a sufficiently coherent and stable stage upon which to develop themselves. Above all, he had not been able to master his society's transition from its more primitive state to the more complicated forms of political, economic and social representation.

'Ironically, what Bourguiba did for the country turned out to be its undoing,' wrote Sadok Chaabane, the early Minister of Justice who was to become one of the most cogent thinkers of the new Ben Ali regime. 'He liberated the country, not the individual human being, and created institutions devoid of life or spirit. Superimposed structures were propped up with no firm foundation in public conviction or in popular participation. He founded the state apparatus, but in the declining years of his presidency, he monopolised power, turning administration into a bureaucratic, personal instrument that gradually became estranged from people and their aspirations and ended up in isolation. Freedom was gone and the spirit of political competitiveness was thin on the ground. But what had exacerbated matters was the economic centralisation and continuous intervention of the state in all production and marketing sectors, turning the state itself into a huge machinery incapable of motivation, sharing, or mobilisation.'

Habib Ben Yahia said to me poignantly many years later, 'We were on the brink of catastrophe, because of the age of the first president, because of his inability to lead, because of his age and sickness. Then all of a sudden, we made it. In a very civilized way, the old man retired, with dignity and respect. History repeats itself: in 1957, the old bey was asked to step down and we shifted from royal to republican regime without bloodshed and the bey's sons moved on to become prosperous businessmen.' He paused and smiled. 'That is our way,' he said.

The Mausoleum and Memory of a Supreme Combatant

Monastir is known not only as the fount of Bourguiba's inspiration but also as the site of a 9th century *ribat* or fortress built to protect the people from roaming nomadic tribes and Byzantine warships. It still stands guard over the sea, but today Tunisia reaches outwards with confidence and not inwards from fear. Bourguiba's mausoleum stands today in this 'hometown', which dates from the 8th century. Today, lovely hotels line the beaches of Monastir and on one downtown circle there is a charming golden statue of Bourguiba as a boy. The child is poised, his young legs seem to be moving ahead almost imperceptibly. There is an expectant look on his face and he is carrying, of course, his books.

No-one knows what went on in the once-brilliant but now thwarted mind of Habib Bourguiba from the time he was deposed in 1987 until he died in April of 2000; but we do know that he was finally laid peacefully to rest in this beautiful mausoleum in Monastir, where the building and its gracious grounds even today reflect his early life, the years of fight and of fortitude and governance and finally the peacefulness of death.

The building itself is elegant but not ostentatious, with two minarets, a golden dome and two green domes, and Tunisian flags in red and white flying in the breeze up and down the wide walkway to the building. His body lies in state inside, in the middle of a calm pool of water that belies the turbulent and sometimes difficult character of his person and of his life. But it is in the little room behind the casket and the pool, a room open to both, that one finds the true symbols of his life.

The documents of his learning, such as his high school certificate, are duly displayed, alongside his large and elegant desk. Then there are the books, always the revealing books! Although he was an avid reader all his life, in his cabinet there are only a few – but they are truly his. Keeping eternal vigil next to his bier, one finds the written expression of the major streams of modernism that crossed and recrossed the entire Mediterranean, in his age and well before it. There are 15 volumes of *Islam: Enlightening Way of Interpreting the Great Thinkers of Islam* by the great 19th century Tunisian reformer Tahar Ben Achour, the distinguished predecessor of Professor Ben Achour whom I had met in his house on Ben Achour street. Next to them are books by Mustafa Kemal Atatürk, the great reformer of Turkey, who provided Bourguiba, like so many other struggling leaders of developing countries during the 20th century, with the first model of a secular Muslim state. Finally there were the works of Voltaire, Diderot, Rousseau, Saint-Simon, Victor Hugo and Montesquieu, all the French literary and political mentors, the intellects and voices of French freedom who had influenced the Tunisian leader so much.

It was in the soil of these philosophical roots that he had planted himself and his thinking, firmly and creatively. It was from these intellectual wellsprings that he was able to come eventually to his own ideas about what he thought Tunisia could 'absorb' without political and psychological 'indigestion'. It was from them that he had formed first himself and then his country and, for a long time, he had startled the world with his originality.

And then, overnight, he had left the country to a man little known outside Tunisia. The world asked: 'How is this new man, this "man of the intelligence", going to be able to lead Tunisia in time of ongoing troubles? Can he?' The answer to these questions would come rather quickly.

Tunisians were proud of the fact that not a drop of blood was shed in the transferral of power. But although they did not know it at the time, they were already shedding their past in myriad and untold ways. One of the major changes in their attitude was soon to be found in the very different way that they responded to their first president and to their second one.

Abdelbaki Hermassi, the Tunisian social scientist, best explained the difference between the first President of Tunisia, Habib

Bourguiba, and the second. 'If you compare Bourguiba to Ben Ali,' he told me one day when we were trying to piece together the mosaic of modern Tunisia, 'the first president was the severe father, whereas Ben Ali is the protective first son of the family. People looked at Bourguiba from a distance and stood up straight. With Ben Ali, they come up to him and touch him.'

4. From One-Party Rule to Evolutionary Democracy: *To Sons and Daughters*

'We are not doctrinaire. When we have failures or problems that can't be solved, we think harder.'

Habib Ben Yahia

'Strategy today is not a document, but a way of thinking.'
Sadok Chaabane, Tunisian political strategist

The Fallen Combatant and the Rising Nation

Once again, as it had been immediately after independence, Tunisia found itself plunged into looming chaos. It is not too much to say that, without the intelligent intervention and dedicated planning of many Tunisians, the Tunisian experiment might still have failed, for the ten lost years between 1977 and 1987 were expensive years. Once again there was no money, and budget deficits were the order of the day. When the Gulf crisis arose in the summer of 1990 and then, hard on its heels, the Gulf War in the winter of 1991, Tunisia had even more concerns about its neighbours. Algeria was facing a fundamentalist onslaught, while Libya, which had been subject to U.S. sanctions since 1986, was implicated in the inquiries into the Lockerbie bombing.

With all of these challenges, a victory for the Islamist movement would have been the kiss of death for the hope and the ideas that had gone into the building of the modern Tunisian state. Yet in fact, nothing illustrates more cogently and revealingly the personality and psychology of the new president than the manner in which he treated this challenge to Tunisia's political, economic and spiritual cohesion.

From the very beginning, Ben Ali was very different from Bourguiba, and from the very beginning, he was often misinterpreted, particularly in Europe. Because of his background in security and because of his hard line against the Islamists, many on the Left in Europe were critical of the Tunisian experiment. To many of them, despite their ultimate hopelessness and repression, Arab nationalism or Communism seemed so much more exciting and invigorating. To these critics, the new president was an austere, upright, distant man who would surely lay down a tougher line than the Supreme Combatant, and could hardly be expected to concern himself in any depth with questions of economic development, much less those of justice or mercy. A quintessential 'man of the security'.

But those common suppositions turned out to be false. The undeniable fact, at least for those who cared to look beneath the surface, was that it was Bourguiba who was the harsh 'tough-guy' on questions of crime and punishment, particularly when the question was political, and even more particularly when it regarded the Islamists. It was Ben Ali on the other hand, who tended to look at the Islamist problem more as an issue of politics and crime in society than as an affront to his personal being; and it was Ben Ali, from the beginning, who had a serious concern for the links between security and human rights in the modern sense of the concept.

Behind Bourguiba's relentless hatred of the Islamists, as Abdelbaki Hermassi so cogently observed, lay 'the obstinacy of the old anti-clerical leader to free Tunisia from any kind of revival of religion.' Bourguiba seemed to consider such a comeback as a personal revenge against his attempts to shape Tunisia along the lines of the 19th century positivist idealisation of triumphant laicity. The 'eradication of the Islamist poison,' he had said, 'will be the last service I'll render Tunisia.' When many of the fundamentalists were brought to trial in September 1987 on charges of treason, it was the failing Bourguiba who steadfastly and stubbornly refused clemency for the Islamists under death sentence. Several were indeed actually executed. When one of the accused, condemned to death *in absentia*, was captured, it was Bourguiba who demanded a retrial of other fundamentalists who had received lesser sentences.

But Ben Ali was not at all pleased with these extreme measures, nor with the rigid and absolute quality of his predecessor's attitudes. Ben Ali disagreed with Bourguiba over harsh sentences for Ghannouchi, because Bourguiba actually wanted to have him put to death. Even before he became the country's second president, Ben Ali was known as someone who consistently argued for legality and clemency in dealing with the fundamentalists. He pointed out to President Bourguiba not only the illegality, but the severe civic danger, of proceeding along such a hard-line course as the one he was propagating in the trials. Bourguiba however, would broach no protest against his position. It was Ben Ali who sought to establish a dialogue with the trade unions and the Tunisian Human Rights League and who would soon attempt, as a first step, to win the fundamentalists over to the state.

Even when Ben Ali was planning the sad, desperate – and dangerous – action to remove Bourguiba in 1987, he was meticulously careful to use only the National Guard, a militarised police force which had been formed on the model of the French Gendarmerie Nationale, rather than the army itself. As Andrew Borowiec wrote in *Modern Tunisia, A Democratic Apprenticeship*, his comprehensive book on the country: 'Significantly, the army was informed but not asked to participate in the operation. A career soldier trained in French and U.S. military academies, Ben Ali did not want to involve the military in an internal problem that concerned the country's political rather than military establishment as well as the constitution. To him, the task of the armed forces was to defend Tunisia against external enemies.' Still other writers on Tunisia, as well as respected foreign correspondent Borowiec, have pointed out the degree to which Ben Ali, in sharp contrast to what so many in Europe thought of him, was actually meticulous in observing the forms and the substance of institutional division and constitutional correctness. This did not mean there was not still torture in the prisons and sometimes severe mistreatment of those apprehended, but there was nevertheless a serious attempt to establish an institutional framework that would eventually do away with such practices.

In the end, it was a contest between the romantic and the realist. As an independence fighter, the Supreme Combatant lived every moment as though the struggle for independence – and he himself – were illuminated by transcendental forces. As a military man, Ben Ali had always had to make well thought-out, cautious moves and he well understood the cost of revolutionary pleasures. So when it came to the Islamists, he did 'not want martyrs', and instead of punishing the Islamists, his intention was to separate the extremists from the moderates and to bring the latter into the centre of the political process. At the same time, he would attempt to separate himself from the extreme and defiant secularism that Bourguibism had personified for the country. If that did not work, he was prepared to be very tough indeed.

In the end, Ben Ali, the 'new combatant', was a far more practical man, a man of the independence struggle certainly, but also a man much more closely identified with the modern age than his predecessor.

At this point, the struggle for the future of the country could have gone many ways, and the success of Tunisia as a modern state was by no means certain.

And Who Was He?

Zine El Abidine Ben Ali was born on September 3, 1936 in Hammam-Sousse, a small town on the central coast. He was one generation removed from Bourguiba, and his family was even less prosperous. He told me there were 11 members of his household, and they often did not have enough to eat. He said to me once, as we sat in his elegant office in Carthage Palace, his voice rising with emotion and resonance, 'I'll give you a confidence.' Then he paused. 'I may at times have violated the laws,' he went on, 'but as Minister of Security, I never arrested anyone who violated the law because his family had to eat. You can verify that with the security. I always tried to put myself in their shoes.' He paused again, then added with a passion that seemed out of character for such a controlled man, 'Even the sight of one poor or unemployed person makes me sick.'

In high school, he was involved in the struggle against French colonialism, and was imprisoned for a time inside Tunisia. But soon Bourguiba's party, the Neo-Destour, saw his talents and sent him to France to be educated for the task of forming the future national army. It was in those years that he trained at the distinguished Inter-Arms School of Saint-Cyr and the Artillery School at Chalons-Sur-Marne, and went to the United States to train at the Senior Intelligence School and the School of Anti-Aircraft Field Artillery. Although Bourguiba had a deeper education in philosophy and political science and was a charismatic speaker, Ben Ali had, beside his military training, a deeper grasp of social reality and a surer instinct for institution-building. With his personal traits of prudence, discretion and clarity, he offered the country a much-needed practical and systematic outlook towards life, an outlook which was broadened considerably during his years abroad as a military attaché in Morocco and Spain, and finally as Ambassador to Poland, where he witnessed first-hand a Communist country in the throes of gradual disintegration.

All his experiences abroad confirmed his belief that there was another way besides the 'popular' ideologies of Arab nationalism and Marxism – as had Bourguiba's years abroad. He also had several experiences in America which, by his own accounts, affected and most probably cemented, his already egalitarian outlook. 'Of course, my stay in the U.S. did influence me,' he told me once. 'One of my major recollections of America was that it was a country that "works", and a people who see work as a system of renumeration.' He paused and smiled, apparently thinking back. 'I had an American friend who would send his child to mow others' lawns for $20. They were well-to-do and they didn't have to do this, but it was to teach the boy that money comes from work, even if you don't need it. That was very inspiring. And in fact, the U.S. is, in general, a great learning school. I try to infuse in my own children the importance of labour and industriousness.' He paused for a moment. 'But I must admit,' he went on, 'that I was surprised that people would send their children to mow lawns for such a small amount. It was a lesson in the ethics of labour.'

He joined the various intelligence services, and rose up the ranks, until he finally became the shrewd and tough-minded head of intelligence. It was then that he found his political vehicle for change.

He never had any patience with extremism; thus while the police (many of them women) who served under him were and are unusually helpful to citizens, they are also known for being extremely tough with anyone even appearing to be a radical. 'Nobody can get away with anything with him,' was the way one minister put it.

It would take some years before the country, and particularly its critics in the outside world, would understand the profound differences between the two men, differences that were rooted in the web of experiences of generations, and which would soon become clear in the style, technique and intention of their speeches and even their interviews.

When it came to speeches, Habib Bourguiba was without parallel. Like other charismatic political leaders, he identified his individual person with his people, and they identified with him. Bourguiba was small, intense, lightly Frenchified in his manners, his eyes always dancing with some idea or other, daring always to provoke and to prod. His deliveries were more soliloquy than speech, lasting sometimes for hours and engaging the people – his people – in every fibre of their being. In many ways, his attitude towards women, virtually unique among that generation of leaders in the Arab world, typified his attitude to his people. It was an image of male virility, of defiance against oppression and, at the same time, of a sense of profound protectiveness. In a sense, he was constantly making love to them.

Ben Ali could hardly be more different. Ben Ali was tall, husky, straight, more somber, with eyes as deep as wells. A handsome, somewhat austere man with a steady gaze and a seemingly deep and unruffled composure, Ben Ali was someone it was hard to imagine wasting hour after hour on speeches. He said what he had to say and moved on – there were things to be done! In fact, Ben Ali's speeches were always short, to the point, logical, orderly and expository. He laid out what had to be accomplished, by the state, by every citizen, and by himself. He could be animated, but his points are not so much causes as rational explanations as to how to manoeuvre the road. His emphasis was not on the personal, as it was with Bourguiba, but on the nation's affairs.

Bourguiba's interviews were also revealing. Princeton University's L. Carl Brown, the most recognised American scholar on Tunisia, recalled in his writings that the Supreme Combatant's interviews with the press were 'like an extended autobiographical deluge.' They 'started with early life and remained... fixed on the pre-independence period.' He was placing Tunisia in the structure of the modern world. Modesty never having been his most prominent quality, Bourguiba gladly gave extended lectures, sat for oral autobiographies, gave weekly addresses that would then be published in books and conference papers. Often he referred to intimate family history, rather in the style of a movie star or a famous pop singer – embarrassingly so to many Tunisians, and particularly for a culture inclined to draw a veil of silence over issues of sex, family and other private matters. Then he would shamelessly merge his own history with the history of the independence movement that was his other great love.

One must indulge in true flights of fancy to imagine a man like Ben Ali ever behaving in such a way. When I interviewed him twice in the 1990s, the first thing that impressed me was the systematic, disciplined and carefully timed manner in which the interviews were conducted, both by him and by his staff.

In the first interview, they had asked for written questions, and at first I demurred. As a correspondent and author, I had grown wearily used to the fact that written questions meant tried, trite and trying answers, and so I usually refused to do this. But for some reason, the first time I interviewed the president, I agreed to put forward written questions. The result was overwhelmingly positive. Not only did he answer each one in a detailed manner, but he answered them in ways so exhaustive and original that I knew they had been written only for our interview.

The pictures of Ben Ali show a distant and authoritative man, and even those who know him seem to sense a certain air of historic Moorish mystery hanging over him. Yet in person, the President was something else. Open, charming, passionate about issues, he was, I discovered, also analytical, computer-crazy and more than a little sentimental about his people, particularly the poor. He listens to others carefully and seems to have the talent of absorbing, and then putting into practice, their ideas. He is not as authoritarian as many of the Arab leaders; but on the other hand, once he has heard everyone out and made a decision, it is made.

The structure of the interview itself illustrated the kind of thinking behind the country's change and charter. It had been carefully crafted beforehand. My questions had been seriously considered, and long and detailed written answers were given to me before I met him. Finally, every question that I had proposed to him was answered very specifically in writing that was concise and comprehensive and which took almost the form of a small book.

I was ushered into a beautiful gold and white salon where he sat in a large chair surrounded by a circle of more chairs. He spoke rather formally at first and, after ten or fifteen minutes, very humorously and informally. In the most interesting part of each interview, I spent over an hour with him together with our translator, sitting in his presidential office. This part was off-the-record and so he could speak more unguardedly – and he did.

What interested me afterwards was the fact that, even though he was very formally dressed on those two occasions, with his ceremonial sash draped elegantly across his chest, and even though he was sitting on gilded chairs in an elegant room, I found it very easy to talk to him. His eyes lit up when he discussed his computers, and he offered to show them to me personally the next time we met, in his family home. In short, he was efficient, he seemed innately thoughtful and, above all, he was business-like.

Other writers who have seriously analysed him, as opposed to those with special political interests, have come out with a similar impression to mine. I. William Zartman, professor of international organisations and conflict resolution, and director of Conflict Management at Johns Hopkins University, wrote in his book, *Tunisia: The Political Economics of Reform* that, 'Ben Ali is in many ways the opposite of Bourguiba: an unassuming not a galvanising speaker, a listener, not an autocrat; a bureaucrat from military intelligence, not a founding father of a party; and a man with a sense of separation of state and party and of civil liberties for citizens. He faced two broad challenges: to assure his own position within the troubled political and social context of Tunisia and to bring about a transition to democracy as his programme.'

The new president's first challenge was to deal with the Islamists, and his first impulse was to grant their parties and their leaders full freedom to take part in political life: he did not want any 'Ramallahs' or 'Gazas,' nor any of those other streets of broken dreams of the Arab world on his watch. Nor did he want all those classic martyrs, with enraged young Tunisians carrying other dead young Tunisians on their shoulders through the streets of Tunis and Sfax. What he wanted to explore was whether the Islamists could and would change once they were inside the political and social 'tent' of modern Tunisia.

Ben Ali's acts were not simply atmospherics. He quickly pushed through a series of pardons and amnesties, emptying the prisons of political prisoners. Death sentences given earlier were commuted to life imprisonment, and no more trials were held. General amnesty laws of July 1989 restored civil rights to more than 5,000 former political prisoners, while fair-minded foreign observers began to note that these acts marked a basic change in the nature of the entire political system, introducing the beginnings of a true system of pluralism and free debate. The desire to take part in the exercise of power and the decision-making process began to explode across society, as the nation's Arab-Islamic identity began to be reconfirmed in a healthy way after many years of marginalisation and foreign cultural influence. And at first, it looked as though the Islamists might actually accept the challenge and change.

When the new government put forward the President's 1988 National Pact, the Islamists proclaimed that they would take part in the new era. The text was signed by the major political forces and national organisations of the country, confirming adherence to the major reforming laws. The radical Islamists changed their name, carefully removing any allusion to Islam, since purely religious parties were by then forbidden in Tunisia. They began to publish a legal newspaper. Two student unions were legally recognised: the General Union of the Students of Tunisia, which was generally Leftist, and the Tunisian General Union of Students, which remained close to the Islamic movement. Many of their activists stood in the 1989 legislative elections as 'independents', insisting, as they told the Tunisian press, that they would 'turn over a new leaf' concerning the past, establish a dialogue 'without any reservations or complexes' and give full support to the country's stability and security. Even the radical Rached Ghannouchi, now released from prison, seemed to be willing to be 'brought around', if only he could be included in power. Many Tunisians breathed a sigh of relief.

But democratic forms and processes are valuable not only as a way in which equal citizens choose their governments, but also cleverly reveal what is so often hidden under the clash of radical rhetoric and nationalistic and religious fervour. In the elections of 1989, the fundamentalists revealed their limited audience when they officially obtained a mere eight percent of the votes (a small 15 percent according to their own tally). Once again, Tunisian developments foreshadowed what would come later, for by the year 2001 and the attacks on New York and Washington by Al Qaeda, much of the same pattern emerged. In all of the countries involved, only a small percentage of the Muslims were radicals, representing probably only one percent of all the Muslims in the world. But they were proving once again, only in a different venue, that their effect on their countries and on the world could be magnified far beyond their numbers by the sheer intensity of the message, and by the sheer fanatic persistence of their spirit.

The small percentage they received in the election however, made the Islamists realise that they would never win in the democratic arena. The hope that they would turn into a true political party ended in near-tragedy, as the same hostile internal movements began to re-emerge to take advantage of the liberalisations of the post-Bourguiba state. Now, serious, open-minded Tunisians began to listen more critically to the words of men like Rached Ghannouchi, who had also clearly said that they wanted not to 'rectify or reform' society but to 'revolutionise it radically from top to bottom'.

By 1990, the Islamists were provoking new confrontations as Saddam Hussein marched into Kuwait and the entire Arab world trembled. By 1991, with the American and moderate Arab participation in the Gulf War against Iraq, the Islamists came out in force with strikes and violent confrontations against police agents within the universities, as terror took over the campuses of Tunis, Sousse and Kairouan. Then, on February 17, 1991, at four o'clock on a dark early morning, a group of Islamists invaded a public building symbolic of the government in Tunis, and set it on fire. As so often happens in history, this single event became symbolic and served to mark the boundaries of past and future. The Islamists had left two civilian guards on night duty, bound hand and foot, to be horribly burned. One died soon afterwards. For the great mass of decent, moderate Tunisians, this event marked an inexorable turning-point. And that spring, when there were still more confrontations, Tunisians were stunned to discover the extent to which the Islamists had been able to infiltrate the army, the national guard and the police.

By September 28, the Tunisian Minister of the Interior announced the discovery of 'an Islamist plan aiming at the seizure of power', and throughout the summer of 1992, trials were held again. With these acts, the Islamists had lost virtually all sympathy among the people, and they were imprisoned or exiled, this time for good.

As the dependable, comprehensive – and critical – *Jeune Afrique* wrote at the time: 'Faced with the fundamentalist threat, real or overestimated by information services, the civil society rallied spontaneously round the government. The intellectual élite hardly showed any sympathy for the Islamists. The middle class, which finally had access to progress, ownership and openness to the world, did not want to see the acquisitions it had gained with difficulties suddenly called into question by political-religious fundamentalism.'

It was in that year, too, that Ben Ali's economic revival, based on loosely regulated private and foreign investment and personal responsibility, achieved a record growth of eight percent, while next door the 'powder keg' of Algeria, its Islamists long allied with the Tunisian ones, was erupting in total civil war. Although few saw it at the time, the Tunisian way of building up people's economic lives as a way of removing the cause and the passions from under the very noses of the revolutionaries, was now beginning to work again, building upon the early years of change. As opposition leader Mohamed Harmel, a former Communist, was quoted later as saying, 'The young used to talk about radical causes, including support for Libya and Iraq, the dream of Arab unity. All that has changed. The political involvement of our youth has collapsed.'

Tunisia was the first country, but surely not the last, to finally see, after all its attempts at involving the radicals in the processes of a democratising state, that the fundamentalists, like the Communists, did not want to 'take part', they wanted to 'take power'. In fact, Tunisia's experience with the Islamists was a direct precursor of what would happen in the years to come, as Islamic radical terrorism rent the world, from the streets of Beirut to the shores of Bali to the towers of New York, and, finally, even the legendary synagogue at Djerba, which was attacked in the aftermath of 9/11. Tunisia faced it first, faced it harshly and faced it realistically but, above all, faced it.

'We are Muslims and proud of it,' Habib ben Yahia said to me one day when we were talking in his office. 'We are profoundly religious people, but we had to clear the picture of those using religion as a Trojan horse to come to power through religious means.' Then, speaking about the Islamist leadership, he recalled, 'They would go to the West and talk about democracy, but we would record the private speeches of their leaders in Paris and London talking about the Islamic republics in Sudan and Iran...'

'It's over,' Abdelbaki Hermassi ruminated another day. 'The Islamists have lost the battle. The battle was waged and won, society tasted them and rejected them. This is a very stable country and a country very much against violence. The Islamists burned two people, and that was the end. In fact, what they wanted was not to participate, but to take over. In Tunisia, they were brought to heel by a multi-faceted approach that combined security handling (dismantling the networks), judicial action (bringing to trial those who had committed terrorist acts), economic action (drying up the springs of their funding), social action (fighting poverty and poor living conditions, where the fundamentalist groups usually recruited their supporters) and lastly by an educational and cultural approach, spreading the culture of toleration, freedom of expression and respect for others' opinions.'

Later, in the spring of 2002, after the world had seen so many similar tests of the fundamentalists' 'good will' from Egypt to Yemen, Algeria to Indonesia, Abdelbaki Hermassi would say to me with thoughtful sadness, reflecting on the events of 9/11 in the United States, 'I used to think there was a modern Islamist 15 years ago, that extremist movements should have an opportunity in the search for power. But I know now that when they talked about human rights, that was only a cover. They were really looking only for the exertion of power. We were alone... nobody listened to us.'

The New Era Begins

Ben Ali's moves were clear, his programmes impeccably defined. To lay the long-term basis for the modern state, he reopened the famous Zeitouna, only now as a separate, state-controlled university in a modern building across town. The school's curriculum was totally changed to include modern topics such as science and economics, and to foster tolerance and critical thinking. Journalists noted, perhaps cynically, that this would not hurt the appeal to foreign investment.

The Minister of National Education, Higher Education and Scientific Research was given the task of putting into place reforms tending towards the 'affirmation of the values of modernity'. He unapologetically removed school manuals which pushed for radical Islamist ideas. Ben Ali now moved to encourage the modern, open, liberal religion that had long been the silent underpinning of the Tunisian form of Islam. He refurbished the old mosques and constructed more than a thousand mosques of every size – a quarter of the total national number. But now there was no longer any place for the radical Islamist preachers, only for traditional religious figures.

Yet what they considered 'true' Islam was still alive and well. Even while all of this was happening, a 'Presidential Award for Memorisation and Recitation of the Koran' was instituted, and the Koran was read non-stop at Zeitouna Mosque every single day of the year. Lectures and study groups for moderate imams and preachers were established, and daily banquets were given for the needy and the disabled every year during Ramadan, to mark the 'real Islam'. The President himself often attended these, to dine and speak with the guests. The governing group knew and appreciated that Tunisia was still a religious country – and should be. There are five calls to prayer each day and the mosques are filled during prayer hours, while instruction in Islam remained compulsory in secondary schools, and television programmes began and ended with a reading of Koranic verses.

They understood one of the many apparent contradictions of containing radicalism, whether political or radical. As one party militant put it, 'the eradication of fundamentalism necessitates the gradual re-Islamisation of the state.' They simply knew they could not sustain, as one minister put it to me, 'religious overdoses'.

A primary example of how they accomplished this was to be found in the 'Arabisation' of the teaching of science and mathematics. As Andrew Borowiec wrote, 'An interesting innovation was the "Arabisation" in the teaching of science and mathematics, under which texts are in Arabic but the figures and symbols of chemical formulae are in standard Latin characters. Consequently, students have to acquire the ability to read the text from right to left and the figures in the opposite direction on the same page. Such a system apparently intrigued several other Arab countries trying to find the best methods of combining Arabic with Western scientific instruction.' Borowiec found that many of the educators he interviewed described such a 'sweeping and modern approach' as emanating from the spirit of the military schools, rather than from traditional academia.

When I personally asked Ben Ali about Islam in my 1998 interview with him at Carthage Palace, he could not have been more clear about his beliefs. 'Islam in Tunisia today is what it always has been, it is the religion of almost all Tunisians,' he said. 'It is a religion of conviviality, love of one's neighbour, moderation and tolerance. There is a clear, unambiguous distinction between Islam and the distorted use that is made of Islam by fundamentalist and terrorist movements. The fundamentalists attempt to exploit religion for exclusively political ends, through double talk and the use of every possible means, including terrorism and violence. Here, as elsewhere, their tactics have been exposed. Just as our fellow citizens are loyal to Islam and its noble values, so they rejected those who sought to seize power by violence and the use of religion.

'But at the same time, and on a parallel track, when you talk about Islam, you have to mention other faiths as well. Our Jewish community for example. Every year, believers come to Djerba and practice their faith in total confidence. All groups, all faiths, are free to practice, including a very small Baha'i community.' Then he repeated his point, as if one could not possibly say it enough times: 'Each person is free to assume any faith he wants.' Another pause.

'But the most important overriding factor is that people work, that they give something in return.'

Those Islamists who had been behind the attacks on the state were now either imprisoned or in exile. Many of them escaped to London and Paris, and used the freedom of the West to broadcast back to Tunisia that women must wear headscarves and that the fundamentalist shari'a law must be imposed upon everyone. This continued to rile the government, which responded with trials of dissidents from time to time that, for their part, angered critics in Europe, where many thought the trials to be unnecessary or unproductive. The important point however, was that radical Islam no longer had any great effect on the people. Their 'experiment' was over. Even the TV station ceased broadcasting shortly after September 11, 2001, when the British and many of the European governments began to clamp down on the radical Islamists they had for so long given sanctuary to.

Tunisia makes a 'Pact' with Itself

What had been implicit under Habib Bourguiba's rule became explicit under Ben Ali. Now, in the country of 'step-by-step', it was time to move on to the next evolutionary phase in its development. In order to encapsulate the ongoing sense of change in Tunisians' minds, the regime first created a new concept and a new title for the age. Next they created the manifesto and the roadmap for it. Finally, they moved systematically to gain the approval of the active strata of Tunisian society and to implement it. These would soon be known as 'The Change' and 'The National Pact'. The idea was to unify the country under a certain number of clear, workable and visionary principles, and to bring the commitments of individuals, labour unions, schools, professional groups and non-governmental organisations together in one unified intention, both for themselves and for the future of the country.

Drawing upon and extending the internal experiences of Tunisia, they forged the new system, which was built upon their own experience of the entire 20th century. But the ideas behind the 'National Pact' were the opposite of the multi-party democracy so favoured by progressive groups in the West. Instead of a process in which differing, and often totally antithetical parties and ideas fight it out at the top, the Pact drew on layer upon layer of interests, groups and ideas in Tunisian society for principles that were debated and delineated at the bottom, prescribed at the top and then subscribed to by society. The Pact set up the rules of the game. These rules were not only extraordinary for a Middle Eastern country, but most probably could never have been achieved in a multi-party society that ruled a developing country from the very beginning, when the competition would have eaten up the time needed to institutionalise the state.

Tunisia would be a pluralist society, women would continue to be totally emancipated, and the state would be dedicated to peaceful and evolutionary, but unrelentingly persistent, social development. It would be a state with Islam as its official religion but one that would assure freedom of religion and would not interfere in people's private lives unless, like the fundamentalists, they tried to impose a violent change upon society. Political change, including freedom for political parties, would be built into the new process. This stage was to be seen as a temporary one, until the Tunisian people had absorbed and digested one level of change and were ready to move on to the next.

The process of the National Pact began, with meetings held all over the country to form a political contract, a written consensus which all protagonists pledged to respect, with teams of young political leaders within the Political Bureau of the Party on hand to launch the rebuilding process. Think-tank committees were set up to explore party ideology, to revitalise political discourse and to lay the basis for the eventuality of pluralist politics.

When the Pact was signed on the first anniversary of the famous November 7 when Habib Bourguiba retired to Monastir, it very specifically laid down these values and principles. The Tunisian state would be based upon: 1) The adoption of democracy, based on intellectual and organisational pluralism. 2) The recognition and respect of the right to difference and a different opinion, plus the protection of the rights of minorities. 3) The adoption of tolerance as a guiding principle of relations between Tunisians and the exclusion of all manifestations of fanticism and violence. 4) The commitment of all Tunisians to strive to go beyond anything that might disunite them in order to create a climate of national solidarity that fosters the reconciliation of all. 5) Tunisia's commitment to its Arab identity and its pledge to promote the Arabic language, while maintaining openness to other languages and cultures, and Tunisia's commitment to Islam as a source of pride and inspiration so as to make it more receptive to the problems of humanity and the issues of modernity. 6) Tunisia's commitment to the Code of Personal Status and supplementary provisions, and the recognition of the reforms embodied therein and affecting family life and women's emancipation.

When I asked President Ben Ali about 'The Change' and the 'National Pact' in the late '90s, he answered: 'We have counted, since we came to power in Tunisia, on the maturity of the Tunisian people. We have proclaimed unhesitatingly that they have reached a degree of awareness and maturity that entitles them to a sophisticated political life... Since 'direct democracy' is a utopian pursuit, we talk with the people through their representatives, whether in parliament or in electoral and professional organisations and institutions...'

I have to note that what I found particularly interesting was his swift and critical reference to 'direct democracy'. Historically, this is the deliberate habit of charismatic leaders like Hitler, Castro and Mussolini, of appearing to go 'directly' to the people and gaining their 'assent' in emotional meetings fraught with dictatorial control of both minds and bodies. The assent, of course, is already assured by the dictators' political and emotional hold over the people. I had myself witnessed it first-hand in Cuba, in the 'Plaza de la Revolucion' when Fidel Castro addressed the Cuban people, employing all of the irresistible and controlling tactics of 'direct democracy', a term that came into being under the similar charismatic dictators in Europe in the '20s and '30s. When he shouted in a kind of ecstasy to the hundreds of thousands sweltering in the heat, 'All in favour, raise your hands,' the people shouted and raised their arms, no longer individuals now but only one great and indivisible breathing amoeba. I found this exchange of powers both fascinating and terrifying.

There is none of the reasoned consent in 'direct democracy' that – at least at best – characterises a real political process, and it was telling that Ben Ali brought that other pattern up so immediately, perhaps because it was so totally antithetical to what the Tunisians were trying to do.

From the moment of The Change and the signing of The National Pact, genuine changes did begin to take place in the inner life of Tunisia, changes that had been impossible under the stern, fatherly hand of Habib Bourguiba. A massive political conference, the first in the new era, called 'The Salvation Congress', was held in July 1988. A Carthage Tolerance Charter was promulgated in 1995, when thinkers and theologians of every religion and creed came together in Carthage. That same year, Pope John Paul II travelled to Tunisia, one of the rare Muslim countries he was to visit, and received a warm and even loving reception. A new law for political parties, which excluded any ideology of extremism, was passed. Amnesty International opened an office in Tunisia in April 1988, the first of its kind in the Arab region, and Ben Ali hosted the Arab Institute for Human Rights in March 1989: no other country in the region had been willing to host it. Critics complained that these were 'tame' organisations, but in fact they represented a step far beyond anything that had existed before.

All the while, Ben Ali was doing his best to bring personalities and opposition figures to his party. He wanted to be 'President of all Tunisians' and he also wanted a 'presidential majority' into which he could co-opt opponents. Always cognisant of the 'religious problem', the law on political parties specifically included a section providing that, 'no party is entitled to make reference either in its principles, its objectives, its action or its programme, to religion, to language, to race or to region.'

Tunisia was beginning a massive, tectonic shift, whose ultimate geostrategic form would not be visible for some time. As I. William Zartman has written: 'The shift from single-party to multi-party rule is a traumatic moment in a nation's history... Works on transitions from authoritarian rule towards democracy have identified a certain number of elements in the process... These are defined as the opening and undermining of the authoritarian order, the establishment of new pacts and the rules of the new game, the restructuring of civil society and public space and the organisation of participation and elections. The essential nature of the process is to turn politics from a private to a public process and therefore to organise and reconstitute the components of that shift. Included in that process must be the establishment of safeguards that politics not be re-privatised, that is, that public participation in politics not end with the selection of leaders who then proceed to do politics privately...'

'When we started in 1987-88, we discussed with the political parties what the democratic debate should ponder,' Habib Ben Yahia told me in one of our interviews. 'It would be a waste of time to debate who is more Muslim than whom. The nationalistic approach? We've seen what it led to! Yet the sacred aspect of our nationhood is not to be questioned. This debate translated into laws explaining why religious parties should be forbidden. We have learned a great lesson from history. From the civil war next door in Algeria, to the Weimar Republic, to the Islamic republic in Sudan... At the same time, 9,000 Tunisians go to Mecca each year, and the call to prayer is on TV every day. We are a very religious nation.'

Strategy is a Way of Thinking

One day, I went to see Sadok Chaabane, a charming and serious man who was Director General of the Tunisian Institute for Strategic Studies, and would later become the influential Minister of Higher Education, Scientific Research and Technology.

To be honest, I was not overwhelmingly interested in the idea of this interview. I had been working hard and it was one of those gleaming, magical days in Tunisia. The beautiful seashores of La Marsa were calling, and the glorious blue and white alleyways of Sidi Bou Said were crying out, 'come for a coffee at the café, come and take a walk along the cliff overlooking the sea, it is a particularly translucent blue today!'

Well, of course, I thought, the interview will be interesting, but we are talking about 'strategy', and Tunisia is not exactly a world military power, so what could possibly be interesting enough to divert me from my other, more engrossing tasks? After all, the very words, 'strategic studies' meant military power and prowess. I was prepared to be presented with a map showing the Libyan threat to the east and the Algerian terrorist threat to the west. (The north, with Sicily only a mere 80 miles away, seemed safe enough, but then again, who really knows?) But I was being fooled by the word 'strategic.' We think we know what it means, in fact we know very little – at least about the new and original sense in which the Tunisians are using it.

What I found was an institute, housed in simple, business-like offices. It had been set up at the beginning of Ben Ali's first administration at a time when the regime was trying to institutionalise The Change and The National Pact. Ostensibly, the institute worked with water management, the 'technology of information' and employment. It dealt with practical, everyday problems, things you could, for the most part, grasp in your hands. So far so good, although I still couldn't quite work out what it all had to do with defeating the Libyans, the Algerians or the Italians.

'Strategy today is not a document, but a way of thinking,' Sadok Chaabane began. 'The main task of this institute is to promote strategic thinking, whether in business, government or the individual. We are trying to create a culture of strategic thinking.'

He then referred back immediately to the important question of transition for countries like his, which were going through transitions from authoritarian regimes to forms of democratic rule. Then I began to understand. 'The thesis is that one-party systems left a political vacuum, so that any democratic transition had to be carried out carefully, or else extremist movements would jump in to fill the vacuum,' he went on. 'Ben Ali has taken measures to make the transition as smooth as possible. The major characteristic of the present period is that changes are taking place at a very fast pace; they affect a lot of areas at the same time. One major effort has been to understand the process of change, to anticipate it and to understand how to deal with it.

'Our first task is to set up a network within the administration and to identify specific areas of study in depth. If you don't know what lies ahead, you may not be training people in the right skills. Since you can't always make predictions, it comes down to how to create a system flexible enough to adapt. A strategy cannot be simply a document, because a document becomes static even while you are thinking about it.'

He then went into the nuts and bolts of their work, which explained their idea of 'strategy'. 'The Institute doesn't do things,' he said, 'it has things done for it. Water, for instance. That would be studied first by the Minister of Agriculture and then we would find out how best to use the resource. Here, as in many parts of the world, 80 percent of our water now goes on irrigation, so we must ask what is the best economic way to use it? At the same time, the institute seeks to be informed about what is being done in the rest of the world to adapt new technologies. Or, take the problem of energy, which is another concern of the institute, particularly with regard to transportation. Tunisia is not an energy-rich country, but it is still possible to find new sources, so it encourages foreign investors to look for gas and oil and gives permits that cover most of the country. It is also in the process of privatising related economic activities, including the production of power. We are also participating in the setting up of distribution networks at Mediterranean levels, involving information, communications technology, phones and computers. We are studying how to promote infrastructure, how to link education, research and health... This is particularly important for Tunisia...'

Then he talked about the main problem that would shake the Arab world by the turn of the century and send so many into terrorist movements across the globe. The greatest challenge for the entire Arab world was not that it did not have educated people, but that it had lots of bright young people without jobs. The difference in Tunisia was that, unlike the other countries, his country understood that it had this problem and that it had to do something about it.

But there was something far more important than the nuts and bolts alone. 'As a result of the strategy,' he said, 'we are also able to avoid making the mistakes of other countries.' The institute was following all the reports in Europe and around the world, adapting ideas and programmes, and studying experts of many different nationalities. But the main task of the institute was to promote 'strategic thinking', whether in business, government or individual initiative. Business in particular had to have a 'culture of strategic thinking.' This meant predicting new technologies, trying to foresee what new industries would or could emerge as a result of those technologies and then attempting to formulate the numbers of jobs that could result from those industries, in addition to adapting the education system to facilitate them.

I thought afterwards that, during the 20th century, certain thinkers and politicians had begun to look at societies as organisms which, like human bodies or chemical mixtures, could be treated and formed almost at will. When Karl Marx developed his theory of societies as purely economic organisms, he waged war in the name of pure 'economic determinism' and sacrificed without a second thought, tens of millions to the illusion. Newer Marxist leaders like Fidel Castro followed him with their own 'ideas' – Castro actually formed groups of psychologists and sociologists to take the rebellion 'temperature' of his people. But when they became too frustrated with the 'Lider Maximo' and his cockamamie economic schemes that condemned them, if not him, to eternal poverty, he would use his gauge to stage massive boatlifts or 'escape hatches' for his mistakes. The Mariel Boatlift of 1980, in which thousands of Cubans fled the island, was one. Other social engineers followed, even in the West.

But the strategic thinking that I was seeing in Tunisia could not have been more different. It was the strategic thinking of an evolving democratic, free enterprise system, linking together and integrating all of the political, social, economic, psychological and metaphysical factors that, when brought together intelligently and creatively, allow a people to change for the better. I suddenly realised that what I was seeing was one of the very first countries to understand modernisation as a science, and culture as the art that supported the science. In Tunisia, the political had become the economic and the economic had become what they call 'political economy', for in modern societies, one factor cannot be isolated from the other.

As the Tunisians often pointed out, the United States went through a similar process for 400 years, but it was a natural and organic process with a step forward on, say, human rights, building upon the previous one. It was for the most part an unconscious process in the West, but today, countries like Tunisia, in what had been considered the Third World, had to design the process, then carry it through overnight and do it consciously and deliberately. Whether it was in Tunisia, Singapore, Taiwan or even post-Soviet Russia, all had to inject principles of modernisation laterally into their societies and then prepare the 'body' of their people for these foreign injections so there would not be a traumatic, pathological rejection of the new principles.

'We discuss security and dialogue not in military terms,' Habib Ben Yahia said, as we discussed this entire new process in the developing world, 'but in terms of sources of security, which are multi-dimensional. All of the concepts of economics and security are tackled in a global way.'

'The President is someone who likes to see long-term strategies,' Sadok Chaabane summed up, 'and he is very good at that. This institute serves as a kind of framework in which people can come from afar and discuss certain issues.' He paused, then added something very important. 'What distinguishes advanced societies from primitive ones,' he said, 'is the ability to think ahead and manage.'

5. A Cultural Evolution: *Throwing Light at the Shadows*

'Culture is the mother; institutions are the children.'

Daniel Etounga-Manguelle, Cameroonian-born President and founder of SADEG, the Franco-African development group

Cultural Revolution and the Modern Age

Soon after my first trip to Tunisia, when officials and élites began to talk to me about 'culture' and to link it to the broader strategic thinking of the regime, my first response was to pull back and think, 'Oh no, not again!' This was an unthinking response, I admit, but it was one formed by the raw experiences of our era, which had too often turned the hoary concept of 'culture' into an ominous vehicle for the most intricate forms of mental and intellectual oppression.

My generation, after all, had been through the horrors of 'The Great Proletarian Cultural Revolution' in China in the late 1960s and early '70s. Culture was to be 'purified' by sending thousands of Red Guards against 'bourgeois power holders' and forcing them violently and often fatally 'back to the countryside' to live with 'the people'. That nightmare only ended, of course, after tens of thousands of lives had been sacrificed, much of the great ancient Chinese culture had been destroyed and an entire generation was left pitifully without any education at all. Then in 1979, out of the most ancient annals of Persian history stepped the Ayatollah Khomeini, with his obsessive vision of a pure Islamic Shi'ite state. It was a purity that soon proclaimed the first fundamentalist Islamic state in the Middle East and led to a generation of war and slaughter without parallel even in modern Middle Eastern history. Long before these bestial examples, indeed from 1917 onwards, came the sordid and tragic destruction of the true cultures of the peoples and republics of the Soviet Union by 'Soviet Marxist culture', culminating at its end in 1991 in a vast, empty, soulless Communist state.

By that time in the Balkans, the Serbs were busy burning mosques, bombing churches in Croatia and destroying the great historic libraries in Bosnia, while the Taliban in Afghanistan, no doubt inspired by all of these these examples of 'cultural terrorism', was chipping away at and finally dynamiting the great statues of Buddha that had stood in the valleys of eastern Afghanistan for 3,000 years.

While all of this destruction was taking place across the world, I was discovering society after society in which the people themselves were left, after the vandals had moved on, with withered human capacities and the nameless terror of empty souls. There was no putting the cultural and psychological humpty-dumpty of the human race together again once it had been broken, for the roots and veins that link the tree or the body to the past were severed for good. This was unquestionably the single most horrifying development that I was covering, and so even the very mention of 'culture' in tandem with public policy immediately raised a 'Danger Ahead!' sign in my mind.

There was the added factor that, in the West and particularly in the United States with its predominant utilitarian ethic, a great debate on 'culture' and development was also ensuing. The more historically-oriented analysts argued that you cannot develop a people without protecting, nourishing and applying their cultural roots, because as the African scholar Daniel Etounga-Manguelle has written, the institutions of a state or society must always take the form of the roots, the habits and the mores of the societies that inspired them. But the other proudly 'practical' school dismissed culture completely, treating it as simply a bothersome diversion from its own viewpoint, which is that everything in life flows from the economic alone. Perhaps the American intellectual Daniel Patrick Moynihan best captured the conundrum, when he said, 'The central conservative truth is that it is culture, not politics, that determines the success of a society. The central liberal truth is that politics can change a culture and save it from itself.'

With these thoughts in my mind, it was with some hesitation that I first listened to the Tunisians. Much of the early discussion in Tunisia about what they were doing in terms of culture was fairly straightforward. It revolved around the rebuilding of destroyed national monuments and the restoration of the memory of prominent historical personalities. They were going to revive the memory of Hannibal for example, and his hundreds of poor elephants, forced to assault the wintry Alps with their ungainly figures. They were going to rebuild the Punic port of Carthage and revive the memory of Saint Augustine. They were working with the United Nations Educational, Scientific and Cultural Organisation (UNESCO) to create an archaeological park on the Mediterranean, including Carthage and Sidi Bou Said. They were going to 'make these monuments live again' through events like sound-and-light spectacles and, interestingly, they were making plans for 'cultural tourism', which would focus tourists' attention on the glorious historic spots of the country, as well as forming 'Hannibal Clubs' among diplomats and officials of other countries as a vehicle for making Tunisia known and appreciated abroad.

My initial involuntary response to any talk of a state dealing with culture, I immediately realised, was totally inappropriate to this civilised country. I would soon find, too, that in culture, as in so many other areas of life, the Tunisians had their own distinct terminology. Although various Tunisians had spoken to me, always with vibrant enthusiasm, about their 'cultural renaissance' or their 'small enlightenment', I first began really to understand those terms one spring day in 1999.

Once again that day, I found myself battling the will of my lesser angels, who were calling me to the beautiful seashores. Still, eventually

I agreed to attend the meeting of the National Day of Culture at Carthage Palace. The President was going to speak and, given my experience with special celebrations like this in the Arab world, I was expecting a long and tedious day. In short, I went to the meeting with great hesitation, but I emerged an hour and a half later feeling quite different. I was amazed, I was amused, I was bemused and above all I realised that nowhere else in the Arab world had I ever seen anything quite like this!

The meeting was held in a spacious, elegant, gilded room, filled with several hundred of Tunisia's finest artistic, film and literary talent, who had gathered well before the appointed hour for the big annual awards ceremony. What immediately struck me was not that they were themselves so elegant and so ready for repartee, for intellectual and cultural élites everywhere in the world tend to have that same poise and posture. What struck me first was that they all seemed to actually like one another so much. The spirit of the day was nothing less than exuberant, with colleagues in creativity playfully jousting with one another and applauding their peers. (Surely never exactly a 'given' with intellectuals anywhere!)

As I looked around the crowded, buzzing room that day, I could not help thinking that 20 years ago, or even ten years ago, all of these creative figures in the Arab world would have been ideologically on some horizon of the Far Left; most probably they would have been Marxists, or at the very least, Arab nationalists who simply abhorred their governments, no matter what kind they were. In addition, any meeting like this would be drawn out endlessly. It would never have started on time and it would have seemed never to end, either. The President, when and if he came, would have been fawned upon in his presence and then brutally ridiculed and defamed in privacy afterwards. On top of that, whatever he said would have been irrelevant, platitudinous and utterly self-serving. I was ready for bed before I even began.

But Ben Ali spoke for just 12 minutes. The entire event moved swiftly and finished in exactly 50 minutes. Who could believe it? A major award was, to the surprise of us foreign visitors, given to an eminently bourgeois insurance company (more about that later). Even more surprisingly, we discovered that a president of a still 'developing' nation could actually have something important, even subtle and sophisticated, to say.

'You are certainly aware of the increasing importance of culture in facing up to the challenges and stakes brought about by globalisation,' Ben Ali began, at exactly 11 o'clock that morning, as he stood on the podium before the group. 'The first of these challenges is none other than ensuring our civilisation and our history the place they deserve in the context of an extremely lively rivalry of cultures.' He spoke of how the small enlightenment, 'cannot be achieved through declarations of principle, slogans or ideological discourse.' He said that it cannot be won through a country's pulling down drawbridges against the future, or by rigid attachment to the past, but rather, 'through our endeavour to make our culture into one that is universally active and... lucidly assimilating those constant values that are common to the various world cultures.'

To my immense surprise, the audience listened not so much out of formal respect as out of genuine interest. 'Culture is an industry in the economic sense of the term,' he said. 'It is also one of the factors for development. As the weight of the service sector increases in international trade, and as communications networks multiply and intersect with one another, culture's importance grows, not only from the point of view of the value that cultural products and articles represent therein, but also because the images, sounds and words carried by communication and the exchanges through the channel of these networks need references and sources, and these can only be found in active, influential cultures. It is because we are aware of these basic implications of world change that we have, throughout these past years, worked constantly to strengthen incentives and mechanisms of support for cultural production, and stimulate partnership and investment in this sector... We have moreover, introduced suitable laws and incentives to allow culture to throw off the shackles of the 'state support mindset' and encourage capital to invest in its various sectors.'

And the small mystery of the insurance company? It turned out that this company had, on its own initiative, begun a contest to reward literary excellence, so it was itself cited by the state. The award, some sort of engraved red pillow, was presented by a military officer, once again illustrating the unusual contacts and unity between the various sectors of society that are, at least in most countries, considered at best antithetical to one another's interests. This is an important part of the 'Tunisian Way', which means handing responsibility over to individuals and to the private sector as fast as the government can do so, thereby actually removing it from the government's power as it diversifies. This has been a conscious and deliberate process that stems from at least the late 1980s in Tunisia, of reaching for inspiration back into the multiple and richly layered cultural heritage of the country – Berber, Carthaginian, Roman, Arab-Muslim, Moorish, Djerban-Jewish, French, Italian and Spanish, and embodied in such famous names as Carthage, Kairouan, Hannibal, Saint Augustine and Ibn Khaldun. It has meant the state giving help and funding to the arts on all levels, so that the social, cultural, and economic elements of society can interact with one another in order to be reinterpreted as the basis for the new age. Finally, it has involved setting them free and encouraging the private sector to fund and sponsor them, together with the artists and creators themselves.

Abdelbaki Hermassi, the sociologist, told me after the awards ceremony, 'The President's speech ties culture to development, to identity. But it is up to the creator to develop that culture. We have here a people finding themselves, creating a theatre and a culture that reflects people's aspirations. We are creating a film industry in which people can find themselves, where young people suddenly say, "That's us!" We are facing our reality and it's a lot of fun. We are trying to reward economic enterprises that encourage culture, and we're inviting the private sector to join in, to put some of their resources at the disposal of the arts. We are saying that culture is everybody's business. The state has an obligation, but it is up to the two crucial sectors to play their roles. We want the creators to be the entrepreneurs.'

With the state playing such an important role in culture, what did that mean for censorship? 'This is not a country known for censure,' he went on. 'In our films, there is absolutely no censorship whatsoever. But that does not mean that there are no sacred values. One can play with ideas, but people must respect the sacred symbols of the country, like the constitutional order or the religious moral order. Aside from things sacred, there is criticism everywhere.'

Or, as Ben Ali said to me, in one of his unmistakable moments of 'don't contradict me please, because this is what I really mean' that arose during our interviews from time to time: 'The state cannot ever be a cultural creator!'

In practice this means that Tunisian films, which are being recognised across the Arab, and increasingly the Western world for their excellence, their charm and their accessibility to the human character above ideology or religion, almost always deal with personal matters, with home and family. But they will also take on such taboo subjects as tribalism and the 'shadow areas' of Tunisia, which neighbouring countries like Algeria will not touch. Tunisian films do not in general delve into political matters, nor do they directly criticise the government.

Another late afternoon, Abdelbaki Hermassi and I were finishing an interview in his office in downtown Tunis. At about 5 o'clock, he looked at his watch and said to me, 'I want to take you to a meeting at the artists' house. Come along, you'll find it interesting.' It turned out to be just that. The meeting – a small celebration really – was held in one of the medina's most exquisite old houses, covered with gorgeous tiles, Cordoban stripes and latticework.

What was most interesting was the interaction between the artistic and creative élites and the politicians. As everywhere, these cultural figures tended to be physically lithe and lean, rather like graceful long-legged birds that had suddenly come to perch on the beach, theatrically ruffling and unruffling their wings and posing in the sunlight for all to see. The politicians tended to look, well, much like your ward politicians of Chicago, all short and squat and not like any bird at all. But what was so amazing, again, was how much they liked one another. All these different mentalities and metabolisms were hugging one another and laughing at the same jokes. They seemed more like partners or colleagues, brothers and sisters, or friendly and respectful adversaries, than protagonists potentially divided by differing interests in a complicated national saga.

I could not help but think that night after I went back to my hotel: 'Is this how the rest of the Arab world could be?'

The Search for Maintaining Identity

From the very beginning, Bourguiba had realised the need to strengthen Tunisian culture or risk the anomie, imbalance and purposelessness that had afflicted so many new countries in the throes of independence and development. He knew that the period after the colonisers left would be the most dangerous of all, for it was at that moment that people were inevitably left with a yawning emptiness, made more onerous by the fact that the formerly dominant culture had for so long devalued and even debased the native culture.

So it was that in 1964, during the first years of his presidency, Bourguiba called his party leaders together and told them that, 'In order to set national sentiment on firm foundations, we must also give the people a full picture of their past, that is to say, the history of the generations that preceded them.' Then he pushed through historical studies in what would mark the beginning and the basis of the new educational reforms on three levels: interpretive scientific studies on the scholarly level in Arabic and French, textbooks for secondary schools showing the broad lines of Tunisian history, and popular publications for the general reader. These lay the basis for the cultural evolution that would come.

When Ben Ali became president in 1987, he addressed the question with even greater passion and judgment. He and his team said over and over again that, because Tunisia was so open – and because it was so determined to be and to remain open – Tunisians needed, even more than in a closed or hermetic culture, to know themselves. He felt that they could not interact with the rest of the world without being in danger of losing themselves, unless they had a solid inner knowledge of where they had come from and who they really were. If they strayed too far from their roots, the entire carefully balanced process of the country could collapse, perhaps from the failure of just one element in the formula. There was always the fear that the country could be catapulted into the violent emptiness of so much of the world, which to Tunisian thinkers had moved too fast and too promiscuously towards the modern lotus eaters' mantra of 'Change, Now!'

Culture was not only desirable for itself, for its own beauty and as a record of mankind's path here on earth, but for the fact that it could become the replacement for closed and fanatical ideologies. Just as Bourguiba had been specific about political theory and about denying Marxism's internationalist pretensions, insisting upon a 'specificity' or a purely Tunisian political model, so was Ben Ali similarly specific about Tunisian culture. 'Globalisation,' he said once, 'does not mean assimilation, just as specificity does not mean isolation or withdrawal. "Cultural specificity" is a fact which we believe in, and which we make use of for the benefit of humanity and for the promotion of a common struggle for excellence, contribution and variation.' He would employ the most modern technology – computers, for instance – in spreading Tunisian culture, but he would be very conservative about preserving the genuineness of that culture.

Meanwhile, former backwater Tunis was becoming such an exciting new centre of culture in the Middle East that by the 1990s it was challenging Cairo and Beirut for the title of 'Cultural Capital of the Arab World'. The Tunisian School of Theatre soon became world-famous. Artists, festivals and celebrations were brought to Tunisia from around the world. Michael Jackson gave a concert in the name of the 'solidarity of the Tunisian people', and other equally unlikely 'stars' now gladly put Tunis on their schedules. In sport, Tunisia suddenly started to win all kinds of competitions in Africa and in other parts of the world. In geopolitical terms, the very same Arab League that Bourguiba had squabbled with so endlessly, moved to Tunis after the Gulf War, because of the endless squabbling among the other members over the war. The Palestine Liberation Organisation, meanwhile, had been in Tunis since 1982 after it had been thrown out of Lebanon. The capital, with its modernity and its moderation, was becoming a vital centre of the Middle East, the one place where industries and institutions were safe to do business.

Tunisia had already revived its education system by bringing back the country's rich, but long forgotten pre-Islamic past – Carthaginian, Roman, Moorish, Christian and Jewish. The key identifying words were modernity, identity and authenticity. Tunisian academies began doing more translations of world literature than any country in the Arab world. And in Hammamet, one of the loveliest of the necklace-of-pearls cities on the eastern coast, is an exquiste International Cultural Centre, a white dream of cubist rooms surrounded by flowering gardens overlooking the blue sea, where international artists and scholars attend conferences and seminars and debate the serious issues of the day.

'It is a wonderful feeling, to be in the avant garde, to be totally involved in our history but also to belong to the whole Mediterranean space.' Bochra Malki, a beautiful and talented Tunisian who worked for the Tunisian External Communication Agency, exuberantly described her feelings to me, feelings that I found to be common among Tunisians today. Then she added something very Tunisian indeed. 'Soon,' she said, referring to the 'shadow areas' of the remaining areas of poverty and backwardness in the country, 'there will be no more "dark spots".

But before I got to those 'dark spots', in order to see for myself exactly what Tunisia was doing in the area of culture, I drove out to the seaside near Carthage to visit the Tunisian Academy of Beit-al-Hikma. This was the private estate of one of the princely families, until the republic was declared. Then, in 1983, it was put at the disposal of the academics. Sitting so intimately on the edge of the sea that you can actually hear the crash of the waves inside the exquisitely decorated rooms, this is one of the most beautiful beylical palaces in Tunisia and bore witness to many great historic moments.

The French Premier Pierre Mendès France spoke here in 1954, acknowledging for the first time the right of Tunisia to its independence. The signing of the code of personal status, which promulgated the daring act of freeing women, was signed here. And when the last bey, Lamine Bey, departed in 1957 and power was given to the republic, it was from here that he left.

My beloved mother, who was a trained artist and had beautiful taste, but who was also a housewife forced to think about practical affairs, would often ask, faced with the most gorgeous of homes, 'Is it difficult to dust?' Only when assured that it was not, could she fully turn her attention to admiring the artistry. That day for some reason, although awed by the magical beauty of the place, I asked the charming head of the academy, a cultivated scholar named Abdelwahab Bouhdiba: 'Is it difficult to keep up?'

He seemed amused. In fact, he smiled an almost beatific smile. 'It is a great honour for us to keep it up,' he answered. 'I think one day here without intellectual activity is a lost day. It is an honour for us to make our academy a centre of scientific and artistic activity. We always try to combine the two, because our academy is interested in the sciences, in literature and in art.'

He then explained the rather astonishing work that the academy was doing, especially for the Arab world today. The work focuses heavily on publishing ('our patrimony', he called it) and on tasks such as translating into Arabic early Middle Eastern scholars like the Roman Catholic Saint Augustine and the Muslim Averroes. International meetings are held every spring, bringing together eminent thinkers from East and West to discuss the important themes of mankind; religion, economic culture and the nature of knowledge and wisdom in today's world. The institute has published many of the main intellectual works of the West, as well as extracts of important texts translated into Arabic, English, French and Spanish. The institute has good relations with other Arab universities like those of Cairo, Damascus and Amman, and its scholars work with Egypt, Lebanon, Iran, the United Arab Emirates, Albania and often too with the European universities.

Did he see their work as being part of the tradition of those great centres of learning throughout history? 'Yes,' he said, his voice rising in enthusiasm as he spoke, 'but ours is a universal model. It follows the European model and touches upon all literature. For instance, we are planning a volume of German literature. For the first time, the work of some of the greatest poets and writers between AD 1050 and 2000 are to be translated into Arabic. Writers like Günther Grass will be accessible to Arab leaders. It is a door we are opening into German literature...'

Once again, it struck me that Tunisia had long been involved in exactly the kinds of reforms that, particularly after 9/11, serious Arab élites, not to mention the West, were pressing upon a still largely unresponsive Arab world. Yet so few knew the Tunisian story.

Sisters of Ben Ali
In order to try and understand more deeply whole question of the place and the importance of culture in Tunisia, I went downtown one afternoon to visit one of Tunisia's most successful young dancers, a

gracefully theatrical young woman named Sihem Belkhoja, who was a director and producer of the Ecole des Arts et du Cinema. I found the beautiful, slim, black-haired young woman in her charming offices, filled with dance and ballet memorabilia and looking very much like a relaxed office in Paris, London or New York. She curled her dancing legs up under her on a chair as she talked with relish and joy about her profession, her mission and her calling.

'I can't give you the recipe for Tunisian success in the arts,' she began, 'but I can give you the personal experience of an artist.' She pursed her lips thoughtfully. 'Maybe I don't have the secret of why, but I do have the chance of living in a country where everything is right. I don't have to fight to remove the veil. I was a dancer and played the violin.' She laughed. 'I was wearing a bikini in the '50s, so I said to myself, is this Tunisia which has given the opportunity to all artists to be independent and free. That is what is really important for an artist, to be free – for it is out of differences that we create things.'

Then, astonishingly for the Arab world – I found myself listening to an Arab woman and a dancer, speaking passionately for what she believed, which was that she must speak out for men and for male 'emancipation' in the arts. She abruptly stopped her narrative. At that moment, her eyes were blazing. She drew her legs up under her even more tightly and gripped them with her hands as though about to say something very important. Then she proclaimed: 'I am fighting for the rights of the man!' She sputtered the words out almost impudently, as if she intended to plant the statement there regardless, and let those who would challenge or contradict her do so.

Then slowly, she revealed her secret. 'Ever since I was 18, I have been fighting for the right of men in a Muslim society – to dance', she began. 'Yes, I fight for the male. At the age of 18, in studios in New York, I had the opportunity to watch breakdancers and to do contemporary modern dancing. I found that the workshops were full of girls and never did a boy step in. But breakdance and hip-hop are male dances, and now we have 1,500 young people dancing here... with equal numbers of boys and girls.' She paused for a moment to shake her head. 'I never dreamed we would have so many boys,' she added.

Her career would be quite amazing in any country, let alone a seriously Muslim country. She has her own dance school enterprise, which is not subsidised but capitalised through her own efforts and profits; she runs an international dance festival plus festivals of contemporary dancing, creates film projects and has already created a film school. She dreamed of inviting American companies to take part in her efforts, but after 9/11, that didn't quite work out. She is all too aware of Tunisia's troubled history. 'I can tell you,' she said at one point, 'wherever there's a dancer, there's no fundamentalist. Dancing is the best argument against the obscurantist mind. If in the Arab world we could have one dance, there would be no room for Osama bin Laden!'

Before I left that day I asked her what – if any – controls there were from the state on someone like her and her work. She literally scoffed at the idea. 'Look around,' she said. I did. The walls were filled with pictures of creative international stars, some of them quite off-beat to a conservative mind. 'I have no pictures of Ben Ali, and the inspectors of the premises hardly ever come.' She smiled, as though revealing a secret. 'As a matter of fact, they are quite lazy – they don't stay for long when they do come.'

Before I left that day, this charming and talented young woman suddenly began reminiscing, and focusing not forwards, but backwards. Her thoughts went back to the Supreme Combatant, to the era of Habib Bourguiba. 'Even in the '60s,' she said, almost wistfully, 'he set up a culture of the dance, he brought dancing over from Russia.' It was she who had said that Bourguiba was a man who adored women, and who spoke of how he loved to dance, of how he recited poems, and of how he 'wanted to do everything for Tunisia'.

'It was not easy to do at that time,' she said, 'and so he had to impose certain things. Only today can we understand why he did certain things...' Then she drew herself up gracefully and stood at the door, her very being filled with life and verve as we said goodbye. 'We are the children of Bourguiba,' she declared to me, her head held high, 'and the sisters of Ben Ali.'

Brothers of the Tunisian Experiment

It was not only the Tunisians who were gaining from the transformed – and transforming – culture of Tunisia. Correspondent Yaroslav Trofimov of the *Wall Street Journal* captured yet another part of the

Tunisian mosaic in a memorable article published in the paper in the late spring of 2002. When he went to Tunisia, he visited Zeitouna University, the educational part of the mosque that had been moved to a more broadened and state-supported venue. In the article, he analysed both the way in which the mosque-university had changed and how it had affected a young African man, Youssouf Savane, who came from Mali, a predominantly Muslim West African country. This is the Trofimov story.

First, he found the entire idea of Zeitouna amazing. 'Zeitouna is at the centre of the authoritarian Tunisian government's push to become a pioneer of pro-Western secularism in the Arab world,' he began, 'and to keep home-grown, militant Islamist opposition at bay...' But he quickly acknowledged that, 'promoting a modernised version of Islam isn't easy. The government's campaign is outspent by wealthy Islamic schools, charities and satellite-TV stations based in oil-rich Gulf countries such as Saudi Arabia, the United Arab Emirates and Qatar. Worldwide, these groups spend billions of dollars to foster a militant version of the religion, often instilling outright hatred of the West. Tunisia's own militant Islamists have launched a London-based satellite-TV channel – also called *Zeitouna* – that calls Tunisia's efforts to revamp the religion a farce.

'After coming to power in 1987, Mr. Ben Ali, the current president, re-opened Zeitouna as a separate, state-controlled university in a modern building across town. In 1995, the school's curriculum was revamped to introduce more modern topics and encourage critical thinking. While this kind of education might eventually foster opposition to the regime, Mr. Ben Ali apparently felt far more threatened by radical Islamists than by Western-oriented thinking. He also hoped a more Western image would help boost foreign investment for Tunisia's economy, already one of the region's most vibrant. To spread this reformist vision, Tunisia's government picks up the bill for foreign students at Zeitouna, including a $40 monthly stipend. About half of the students come from abroad, mostly sub-Saharan Africa but also countries as far away as Macedonia and Indonesia.'

Most of Zeitouna's 2,000 students today, he wrote, were 'preparing to become preachers at mosques or schoolteachers of

Islam' and were 'encouraged to think tolerant thoughts. A rare but prominent exception to the fundamentalist trend sweeping the Arab world, Zeitouna is trying to bring Islam in line with modern society... Zeitouna alumni tend to assume important religious and political roles across Tunisia. For example, some supervise imams who lead prayer sessions at mosques. Many graduates also monitor the mosques to make sure the houses of worship don't turn into hotbeds of anti-government activity.'

He went on to write that, 'Inside Zeitouna's spartan classrooms, women outnumber men and don't wear veils – an unusual sight for an Islamic school. Christianity and Judaism are taught as part of the four-year curriculum, and they are presented as viable religions, not just something to be subjected to Islamic critique. There is a Hebrew-language course, taught by a Muslim woman. To accommodate foreign students, Zeitouna even plans to offer some classes in English and French.'

He quotes the university's president, Mohammed Toumi, whom he notes is 'clean-shaven and wears a suit and tie and refuses to set foot in "unfree" Saudi Arabia,' as saying, 'The Koran has 125 verses that insist on religious freedom and that ask Muslims to respect others.'

Finally, the writer describes two of the foreign students at the new Zeitouna. Mali's Youssouf Savane says that when he first came to Zeitouna, he believed that only Islam held the truth and that other teachings were false, 'I know I was wrong; other religions are just as valid and have their own proofs.' Incredibly for the Middle East, at the university he studied everything from comparative religion to Darwin's theory of evolution to Freudian psychoanalysis. The other student, Diomande Soumaila, from Ivory Coast, says that his classes there set his thinking apart from other students of Islam who had studied at more rigid schools in the Persian Gulf. 'These people think that one must grow a big beard and don a bedouin *dishdasha* to be a good Muslim,' he is quoted as saying. 'Here in Tunis, they teach us to use our own heads, instead of simply following the Koran and the Prophet's sayings.'

At the same time that fundamentalist Islam, in the form of Al Qaeda and other organisations of religious radicalism, were sweeping the world, this was what was happening in Tunisia.

From 26/26 to 21/21 in One Generation

The cultural element within Tunisia never stopped at the narrow water's edge of the strictly artistic and intellectual in terms of art, literature, dance or even the religious and scholarly aspects of human activity. In the Tunisian experience, 'culture' was always connected irrevocably to the larger experience of language, custom, education and the complex of institutionalised traits learned and transmitted by man as a member of society, including the humanitarian. To them, this part of culture, as one Tunisian professor put it to me, involves 'the extraordinary sense of being linked to something strong in Tunisian society in terms of a deep sense of compassion for the excluded, the needy and, in the realm of culture, the giver.'

I was soon to find out that nowhere is this part of the experiment more important than in the 26/26 Programme, begun by the government but funded in good part from contributions by the people themselves. It is a programme which has played a major role in eliminating the poverty that infects the Arab world as well as the entire Third World, and everywhere dulls men's souls and destroys their spirit.

Much as in the ancient era of the Roman *fossa regia*, the great Roman ditch that delineated the boundary between the city-dwellers of the southernmost part of the Roman Empire and the outlaw tribes of the South, in today's Tunisia there is also a line that divides material prosperity (and spiritual enlightenment) from physical poverty (and inclusion in the modern state). The division now is between the vast prospering middle class, which represents about 80 percent of the population, and what the Tunisians call the 'shadow areas'; no longer ethnic or tribal areas, these are in effect isolated rural areas still lacking in basic amenities like running water, electricity, housing, health care, education and roads. These are the poor that are always left behind after the first stages of prosperity and development and that, in most countries, stay left over.

One afternoon in 1997, my friend Oussama Romdhani, the head of the information office in Tunis, urged me to go and see what 26/26 was doing. I am embarrassed to admit that at first I demurred – once again, if truth were to be told, I was having my very own 'lotus eater' dreams. But finally I gave in and, as it turned out, I was glad that I did.

As we drove away from the bustle and business of the city, in the foothills of the mountains only an hour's drive outside Tunis, you could still see some of the miserable shacks of the old Tunisia; mud huts stuck in ever more mud, crawling with insects and without water or light or hope for the better. But now there were only a few of them left. Soon we came to Borj Louzir, a neat and spartan, but attractive, little town of simple white and blue houses where the people who had formerly lived in the shadows had moved into the sunlight. The 13 families in the row of houses that we were visiting were part of the future, my guides told me. The Tunisian government programme is designed for humanitarian, for security and (once again, that revealing word) 'strategic' reasons. We were here to meet one of this era's curious new heroines.

She came towards us like one of those sandstorms in the Sahara. As soon as we arrived, Henia ran at top speed and was upon us. A sparrow-like and rather excitable old Berber lady in her 80s, Henia was wearing old-style tribal robes. Her face was uncovered, but it was hard to make out the details of it, because there were so many kinds of Berber dye painted across her thin, wizened little face. She was surely playing her role, but I was convinced that it was an honest role, if only because it would be difficult to get anyone to pretend to be that enthusiastic. 'Thanks to God and the President, we can call ourselves human beings,' she cried, hugging us all before we visited her simple, modern two-room home, which was clean and neat, with modest modern appliances and a fenced-in private yard. Small, well-tended gardens also edged the road. 'I was living in mud and tin but, thanks to him, we can consider ourselves human,' she shouted.

Then she dragged us into her house and showed us the famous poster of her literally seizing and kissing President Ben Ali when he visited her. In fact, the poster is everywhere around the country, and Henia was well aware of that. 'Look,' she cried loudly, pointing at the picture, 'look at how handsome I am!' Indeed, during our time there, she chirped like a bird in her Berber tongue and one could soon begin to think of her as a creature from some enchanted aviary in the Mediterranean sky.

Poor Ben Ali, he really never had a chance when it came to this lady! It seems that the very first place he investigated after he first grasped the idea for 26/26, he was destined to meet her. (What happened to all the analysts' descriptions of the Tunisians as restrained and moderate people?) Without so much as a 'by your leave', she exercised the prerogative of the elderly lady in any society in the world and did what any red-blooded Berber lady would do. She grabbed the President and kissed him, something that he apparently did not resist. Even in the pictures, which are all over Tunisia, this normally self-controlled man looks more than a little stunned! Old Henia had become the poster girl of 26/26 Tunisia, and dare one say that she truly loves it?

But then, Tunisia has always been highly egalitarian. The country has no titles, no ranks and few pretensions about birth or social scale, although the wonderfully rowdy businessmen of Sfax, a famous commercial centre halfway down the eastern coast, will soon let you know that they are the very best businessmen in the world.

But let us get back to the subject. How did this programme, which is definitely included as part of the cultural renaissance of Tunisia, actually begin? What has it been able to accomplish? Is it applicable to other countries with 'dark' or 'shadow' areas?

In 8th and 9th century Baghdad, there lived a legendary and luxury-loving leader named Harun al-Rashid. He introduced a special kind of practice into Arab and Muslim leadership. In order to find out what was really happening in his realm, or in shadow areas beyond his eye's reach, this fifth caliph of the Abbasid dynasty would sneak out of the palace at night dressed as a common man. Thus disguised, he would visit the *casbahs*, the hospitals and the public buildings to see how the average man was being treated. When it was revealed, either on the spot or later, that it was the monarch himself who had been slighted or cheated, many heads fell and many wrongs were corrected, particularly since, on his nocturnal wanderings, he would often be accompanied by his executioner as well as his favourite poet of the moment. In fact, successful modern monarchs like Sultan Qaboos of Oman and King Abdullah II of Jordan have followed this practice and so, to a less dramatic degree, has Ben Ali (although certainly without either the poet or the executioner). It was a natural practice in countries with vertical authority, where magic and majesty is invested in the monarch.

Thus, in December 1992, five years after he took power on the occasion of Bourguiba's retirement, Ben Ali went to visit two isolated villages, Zouakra and Berrama in the mountainous north-west of the country, and he was shocked by what he saw. Immediately, he ordered the identification of all of the most serious 'points of poverty' in the country, focusing on 200,000 families or approximately one million people out of a population of around seven million.

The name of the programme refers to the bank account number to which individual citizens or groups can make their contributions; many are voluntary but some contributions are taken out of workers' paychecks as well. Today there is a Tunisian Solidarity Bank, which offers preferential loans with low interest rates (not to exceed five percent) for starting up small businesses. Indeed, the contributions have become so widespread that in one day, called a 'National Solidarity Day', one million ordinary Tunisians contributed, thus creating what they like to call a 'culture of solidarity'. By 1997 when I visited Borj Louzir, the massive response of institutions and individuals had created an annual budget of more than $60 million, creating new homes, roads, schools and infirmaries. Complementing this still further are 'restaurants of the heart', which provide free meals to the poor.

But 26/26 was not merely designed to make people feel good, and indeed that is one of the impressive things about the Tunisian social thinking. It is all hard-headedly aimed at results. There is none of the spirit, found in so many countries among well-meaning people, 'Well, at least we tried...' Trying without succeeding is morally and practically disdained in Tunisia. The 26/26 programme, integrated with so many other programmes, is specifically designed to be moral and right, but it also aims to complete the creation of a middle-class society and to create human and social 'antibodies' to radicalism.

Even observers who do not agree with the Tunisian way have to agree that it has achieved much. Poverty has dropped from 22 percent in 1975, to six percent in 1997 and to 4.2 percent in 2002. By the turn of the century, the percentage of Tunisians who owned their own homes had risen to 80 percent – a prime indicator of social stability everywhere, whether in post-Communist Russia, in America or in North Africa. But it is the total effect of all of the programmes together that makes such advances possible, and it exists in the midst of a huge Arab and Muslim world in which poverty is general and ignorance is the general curse.

When you look at some of the terms that the Tunisians use to describe what they are trying to do, you realise how different and how unique this 'way' is for all its imperfections. First there is the evocative image of banishing the 'dark' or the 'shadow' areas, with all that means in terms of shedding light, of rejuvenation and indeed of salvation. Then they speak of the cultural dimension of the policy of The Change and of 'salvaging a section of the population from isolation, allowing them to benefit from their natural right to lead a better life based on dignity and well-being.' Always in the background is the strategic dimension, which is neither military in its primary intention nor aggressive towards others, but only aimed at moving the entire society forward, together, all at once.

By 1998, President Ben Ali told me, the fund's interventions had benefitted 928 areas inhabited by over 151,000 families at a total cost of about $366 million, of which 85 percent was devoted to the provision of utilities, drinking water, electric light, tracks and roads, and the remaining 15 percent to the creation of sources of livelihood in the sectors of agriculture, handicrafts and cottage industries. The 26/26 programme is only one part of a huge scheme of urban and rural housing that the government has embarked upon since the very beginning, backed up by large working programmes of social security and cultural development that caused UNESCO in 1997 to designate Tunis the 'cultural capital of the southern shores of the Mediterranean.'

But what really illustrated the change was the fact that, as the shadow zones were in retreat and the programme was drawing to an end, doubtless due to its good parentage, 26/26 soon had a 'child' of its own. A new fund, the 'National Employment Fund 21/21', was announced in October 1999 and in effect carried 26/26, which will soon have done its job. The new fund was no longer aimed at the poor, if only because even that small number is consistently being diminished, but at young men and women, job-seekers who need to find their way in a more complex world. 'You want to start a business?' one Tunisian interpreter asked me. 'You need computer skills? You come with your ideas and they'll give you micro-credit.' It is for the young, aged 25 to 30. The main idea is to end reliance on the government – you've got to rely on yourself in the long term. Within two years, the fund reported that 41,000 young men and women had been helped to reach salaried or independent jobs, while others were being trained and 3,000 enterprises had been established.

Based on the Tunisian idea that 'employment is a token of human dignity and right and that is at the heart of the social dimension of sustainable development', the fund aims at 'developing the employability of the unemployed' and building into human lives a flexibility for work and for changing employment in a world that is constantly developing. Or, as the interpreter said wisely, 'If someone is educated, he or she can always do something else.'

The transition from 26/26 to 21/21 in one generation, from dealing with problems of extreme poverty to moderating the new problems of opportunity and choices in a rapidly developing world, is what this process is really all about. In Tunisia, this is a process that is working.

Another 'Shadow Zone'?

If there is one cultural zone that has not kept pace with the progress of the rest of society, it is the Tunisian press. Even the authorities complain of the lack of media creativeness, despite all incentives to promote pluralism. Critics point out that too often, headlines will announce the accomplishments of the government – accomplishments that are wonderfully real and can stand on their own – and then announce them again and again. And so instead of the world seeing these accomplishments as an entirely new approach, they make outsiders, who are already critical of Tunisia because of its totally legitimate struggles against the Left and against the Islamists, view it as an authoritarian state.

As Andrew Borowiec has reported in his fair-minded book, 'The President is seen sitting stiffly receiving a foreign dignity, shaking hands with another, or talking to an official from behind his desk. A typical headline in the government French-language daily *La Presse* will be, "Admirable work is being accomplished in Tunisia under the direction of President Ben Ali." Other headlines announce "International consecration of President Ben Ali's actions... Pledge of workers to double their efforts in the face of the economic challenge... Tunisia gives an example in Euro-Mediterranean cooperation," and many other similar jewels of official journalism.' Surely this does not represent the sophistication and complexity of the Tunisian saga, which is as complicated sociologically and geopolitically as a Shakespeare play or a Keynesian economics seminar. There is also a degree of inhibitive self-censorship, not unusual in a country in the throes of development, but it is a degree that must constantly be reassessed, and one that many Tunisian officials privately agree must be replaced with a more modern approach.

On the other hand, as on so many levels in Tunisia, all of this is changing daily before one's very eyes. The best minds in Tunisia today simply bypass the national press and point out that there are lots of debates in the country and this is being widely encouraged through new concepts like televising the parliamentary sessions. There are international newspapers and magazines available just about everywhere in Tunisia, plus a plethora of cyber cafés and every kind of business and social transaction with the outside world, which is becoming closer by the day. The majority of newspapers and magazines, in contrast to the past, are now owned by the private sector, and opposition parties publish their own journals, some of them stridently critical (they also receive state subsidies). Controversies are debated live on television and Tunisia now has one of the most open media landscapes in the Arab world, with figures from 2001 showing that more than 51 percent of households in the Tunis area are equipped with satellite dishes and therefore have unfettered access to all international TV stations. Tunisian entrepreneurs, men and women, travel all over the world, while the European Union, with all of its carefully crafted institutional principles for free expression, is looming on Tunisia's horizon.

President Ben Ali himself criticizes the press for its pusillanimity, insisting that he wants a more active and assertive (if not exactly aggressive) press. He told a meeting of newspaper editors, 'You all print the same articles and the same pictures. Our country today deserves a higher level of information. But the level we have reached is below what I had expected.'

The undeniable fact is that the old Islamist threat is still out there on the geopolitical horizon of the Middle East, as well as on the psychological and emotional horizons of many Tunisians' minds. As the world saw with the attacks on 9/11 and afterwards, Islamic radical fundamentalism is certainly active across the entire Arab and Muslim world. In the final judgment, the simple fact is that a poor press only feeds the criticism of a country's enemies, a wholly unnecessary burden on a country like Tunisia that is in general doing so extraordinarily well.

A Brief Final Thought on Culture

Looking at Tunisia's culture, one can see that the Tunisian experience is a cultural evolution designed to free men, not to enslave or impoverish them, and it was and is exactly the opposite of the other experiences with 'culture' that seemed to poison so much of the world that I was covering. The Tunisians' revival of their own culture was directly designed to root young Tunisians in their own, real and distinguished identity – in their complicated and sometimes ambivalent heroism, in their religious background and in their music, art and literature. This rootedness was not developed in order to divide them from the world but to give them the confidence of being citizens of the world. 'Because we are such an open country, we need to know ourselves,' one minister remarked to me, tellingly.

And so one comes across yet another piece of the mosaic. If this piece of the rich picture had words, it would tell us that above all in development, you should never ignore the cultural. It is the invisible glue that cements together all the other irregular pieces – or it is the missing piece that will silently destroy the whole. It also teaches the world a lesson that many people are quite literally dying to hear, that you can modernise without losing your soul.

6. From Developing Nation to Emerging Nation: *The Politics and Process of Incremental Change*

'It is not enough to enact a law, it has to become reality.'

M. Fethi Merdassi, prominent Tunisian economic strategist

The Days of 1,001 Decisions

By the time I returned to Tunisia in 1999, the country had moved on again, taking another step on the ladder towards prosperity and development and adding innumerable new pieces to the mosaic, which was actually beginning to take form as a coherent work. When I travelled to Carthage Palace to see President Ben Ali and his leading assistants, the government had just announced another plan. It was not a small plan as countries go; it was a five-year plan to move the country still further, as always, at Tunisia's own pace and within its own physical and psychological space.

Many who are attuned to modern economics recoil in horror when they even so much as hear the word 'plan'. Third World 'planning' had in the past too often sounded and looked like Communist planning, and brought back memories of the Great National Plans of the Soviet Union that were passed down from the Soviet planning office, Gosplan, from 1928 onwards, with each enterprise receiving books as large as the Manhattan telephone directory. In these tedious tomes was dourly assembled every detail of what should be produced, what every cog in the machine must do, at what cost and on what time schedule. Not only was there not the slightest provision for personal initiative, but there was no room for the initiative of the manager of the plant nor even for the local Communist leaders. Nothing would ever move or change; it would always and forever remain the same. Not surprisingly, the result was stagnation while the U.S.S.R. was alive, and implosion, national depression and economic meltdown after the Communist state collapsed in 1991.

In Communist countries – or for that matter, in most authoritarian or dictatorial regimes in the Middle East and the Third World – there was virtually always one idea and one true faith. Whether it was Marxist ideology, Arab nationalism, Islamic radical fundamentalism, or just some generic authoritarian dictatorship, the dominating idea was that there was one explanation for life. Such a rigid perception could not be further from the situation in Tunisia, where the truth is always to be found in the 1,001 details of life.

In contrast to those other restrictive plans, the secret of the Tunisian plan was that every step was designed to move the country forward, by giving more responsibility to the company, to the managers and above all to the individual citizen. ('Incremental' was one of Ben Ali's favourite words.)

I had returned to Tunisia in the years of celebrations and change, both in Tunisia and the world. In 1997 in Tunisia, they had celebrated the 200th anniversary of the country's ties with America, the 10th anniversary of the new era's 'Change' and the 20th anniversary of Anwar Sadat's historic trip to Israel. They had noted the 50th anniversary of the creation of the state of Israel in 1947 and the beginnings of the haunting 'Palestinian problem'. In 1998, the United Nations hailed Tunisia as one of the few countries in the world to serve as an international model. U.N. Secretary-General Kofi Annan noted that ten percent of the countries in the world create 90 percent of the world's problems. The international community should not ignore countries like Tunisia, he asserted, which 'raise no problems and set a good example'. Then, in December 2002, the U.N. General Assembly adopted a resolution calling for the creation of a World Solidarity Fund based upon the specific experience of 26/26 and proposed by Ben Ali.

But the 1990s also signalled troubled times elsewhere. Civil wars in Bosnia, Croatia and Kosovo witnessed a resurgent Serb nationalism, not unlike the radical Islamic nationalism in the Arab countries, which resulted in the torture and murder of hundreds of thousands. In the Rwandan conflict between Tutsis and Hutus, at least 900,000 lost their lives, while Central Africa erupted into a seemingly endless civil war of tribe against tribe, militia against militia and fragile civilisation against Hobbesian de-civilisation. Latin America was gamely trying what was essentially the Tunisian way in economics, through liberalising and privatising their economies in what came to be called the 'Washington Consensus'. But this experiment, which stretched across the borders of the western hemisphere, was not destined to work for the very simple reason that, outside of Chile and Costa Rica, both of which largely comprised Central Europeans as their base population, not one of the Latin countries was really willing to commit itself to the patient, persistent creation and construction of the human and physical infrastructure that Tunisia had embarked upon.

Almost every one of the countries in those 1990s horror stories – Serbia, Croatia, Bosnia, Rwanda and Nigeria – had had multi-party elections, most of them several before they descended into their special modern hells. In fact, these elections, arguably coming too soon in the development of many of these countries, constituted one of the factors which allowed single leaders or winning parties to engage in the 'take all' in the pattern that ensued. The Serbian President Slobodan Milosevic for instance, was duly 'elected', allowing him more easily to set ethnic group against ethnic group and to order the slaughter of tens of thousands of people across the Balkans. And so these experiences provide another interesting lesson on the relative unimportance of elections, if the other variables of cultural tolerance, civic society and economic egalitarianism are not equally attended to.

In contrast, the Tunisian example, as I wrote at the time, was 'like a ball of many intricate ribbons, strings and necklaces all tied together.' Later I decided that it was the Middle Eastern nation, not of Baghdad's legendary one thousand and one nights, but of 1,001 small decisions, all intertwined and integrated with one another in infinitely complex and supportive marriages.

The basics remained the same, of course, whether a reliance on private enterprise, the evolution of democratic forms and cultural freedom or the patient building of a workable civil society. The principles also remained the same, whether less reliance on government, the strength of moral culture or building from the bottom up and not, as so many of the failed countries had done, from the top down. But within those principles, there were myriad small but persistent and practical economic changes in the plan.

The educational system would be deepened; women's participation in every part of the nation-state would be further encouraged; one percent of the budget would now go on scientific research, and another one percent on culture; foreign investment, which had already doubled between 1997 and 1998, would be encouraged on every level, along with continued privatisation of industries and commerce, as the government deliberately set itself up to do less rather than more; the country would come closer to food self-sufficiency and water preservation would be enhanced; advanced technologies would be taught and encouraged by the government at every level and the idea of 'lifelong learning' would be vigorously propagated. Programmes were announced to end any remaining unemployment – which was already in single digits – by the year 2004; and technology caravans would carry the latest technology to every unshadowed corner of the country, lest someone be left behind.

And women – always, women! In his speech, President Ben Ali stated unequivocally and in a tone that did not invite contradiction: 'We will make every effort to ensure that women are full partners to men and have equal opportunities to assume responsibilities and be promoted in public life. It is our hope that women win more than 20 per cent of the seats in the councils at the next municipal elections.'

It was all due to 'very detailed and complex programmes', the President explained to me, when we met again in his large and beautiful office at Carthage Palace. He believed passionately in an 'incremental, evolutionary development' in place of the rhetorical 'revolutionary development' that still characterised so many of the failed states all around him. 'My intention was always to change the mindset of the people,' he went on. 'We have had one-party rule and a president-for-life. Now, I'm happy to see a change occuring in the mindset.' He wrote in the formal future plan that even the status of his country was changing as, 'at the end of the 20th century, Tunisia is indeed in the leading pack of "emerging countries". It is already classified among countries that have approached the level of "advanced economies".'

As I left his office that day, an odd but revealing image seemed to be shadowing me. I kept remembering my first trip to the South, when I first saw the Berbers either dug into the very ground of the country in their strange houses, or perched on the cliffsides in their defensive villages; and I thought about how, in this evolving modern state, they were actually having the courage and the security to move down to the valleys, and from there, given the right developmental circumstances and principles, to reach out across the entire world.

And Then There was Europe

In 1995, the country took a staggeringly important step. A mere eight years after The Change, and building upon her steady economic success, Tunisia became the first North African Arab country to sign a marketing agreement with the European Union.

This meant that, by 2007 or 2008, it would have to have its institutions, its regulations and indeed its entire 'political economy' (another of Ben Ali's favourite terms) in line with the European Union's stringent regulations for all of its members. The 'New Europe' was already bringing the developing countries into the European institutions. That meant reforming their entire internal institutional frameworks, and thus their psychologies as well. It reached out and took this small, unbothersome country into the responsibilities of the modern Western world. For the first time, an Arab country could actually follow European countries like Spain, Portugal and Ireland, which had been adopted by the old European Union, had received subsidies and institutional encouragement from the richer and more advanced central European countries, and were now equal partners in European-style modern development. (In some cases, such as Ireland, the new country moved ahead of the levels of the original union.)

The Tunisians would soon be saying that, in a few years, Tunisia might become 'another Portugal', because Portugal's real, but still modest, achievement within the European Union seemed within their reach. Actually, that hope was probably an underestimation of how far they could go, because Tunisia would probably advance beyond Portugal. Still, the newcomers had ahead of them the complex business of what the Union calls *la mise a niveau* or 'coming up to the level' of European standards. That was not an easy process, but one thing was for sure: once assured of the market tie to the European Union, whatever was left of the 'complex of the colonised', never very strong in Tunisia to start with, had now vanished completely.

However, the responsibilities behind the possibilities for change were onerous and the *Financial Times*, for one, predicted that in Tunisia 'the dismantling of tariff barriers will also reduce government revenues and could lead to the collapse of between 15 and 30 percent of Tunisian industry... On the one hand, the European Union agreement heightens the government's apparent feeling of vulnerability, and thus can be used to justify increased levels of caution and vigilance. On the other hand, to overcome these challenges, the agreement also requires the government to move faster on liberalisation, which means reducing the state's hold on the economy and accepting that control will have to be ceded to market forces.'

The public sector's share of value had already gone from 48 percent in 1985 to about 40 percent in 1997, while the state still accounted for more than 60 percent of bank assets, and public enterprises made up about 23 percent of the Gross Domestic Product, according to the World Bank. When one considered 'the neighbourhood', this was little less than astonishing. Both Algeria and Egypt, for instance, which were in line for accession to Europe, had reversed their political liberalisations of the 1980s in the face of bloody and obdurate Islamist challenges, which had sapped all their energies. Egypt then tried to accelerate reforms after 1996, when it had largely defeated its fundamentalist revolt, but these reforms remained only piecemeal, corrupt and largely ineffective.

In short, the Tunisian programme involved a rather staggering process for the rehabilitation of the Tunisian economy by 'deepening the reforms we have undertaken since 1987' as Ben Ali told me in 1998, 'increasing the competence of human resources, modernising the infrastructure and helping the productive sector improve its performance and output both quantitatively and qualitatively.' Then he added thoughtfully, 'The agreement means that the Tunisian economy must raise itself to the level of the European economies in order to acquire the necessary competitiveness and vitality. This agreement... is our bridge to the status of a developed nation.'

The World is Suddenly Very Small

In order to fully understand this crucially important new step for Tunisia, and to assess what these changes could mean, not only for this nation, but for the entire Middle East, I went to see M. Fethi Merdassi, the then Secretary of State and Minister of International Cooperation and Investment. I said, 'Tell me, what is this all about, and please tell me in terms that a consummate non-economist like me can understand.' And he did.

'You know that Tunisia is a small country – we have only nine million people, consumers, so this is a small market for investors,' he began, as we sat in one of Tunisia's revealingly utilitarian economic offices. 'So since 1987, we have made a lot of reforms. We wanted to build an open economy and to create a free trade zone with Europe, which is a very large market indeed with 360 million consumers. So the most important thing for us to know is whether what we produce in Tunisia could be exported to Europe without duties. We had to show our economic competitiveness in many industrial sectors and in the International Monetary Fund and the World Bank. The most important thing for us is that now Tunisia is not a small market but a big market. On July 7, 1995, we signed the treaty with Europe. It's a big challenge for us.

'We do have difficulties, because we are dismantling some industries,' he went on, thoughtfully. 'We can export now without any payment, but European goods still pay some duties here for ten years. Meanwhile, we are opening more and more of our economy and the role of the state is changing. Now, the state is not building any enterprises, it now plays more the role of referee. The private sector has the major role.' He spoke then of the privatisation of 62 public enterprises, with a few more to come in the next few years. Cement plants? The state was getting 'out of business' in cement. Tollroads? These new motorways, so much broader and faster than our little road in the Sahara with the confident white line down the centre, were being built by private companies. They had created their stock market, where you could buy local shares up to 49 percent of the equity of the company (and soon possibly 51 percent). There were advances being made in private agriculture, including hothouse agriculture in the South; there were off-shore industries for France, electronics and mechanical engineering, car components, cables and electrical wares, pharmaceuticals, textiles, upper grade goods, food processing, computers and textiles.

The Tunisians concerned themselves with labour laws, minimum salaries and competitiveness (but not at the cost of women and children being exploited). An innovative tourism agency which pioneered low-cost group tours began bringing Europeans and even Russians to Tunisia in large groups for inexpensive but high-value tours. By the turn of the century, Tunisia's tourism numbers – five million tourists a year – exceeded those of the legendary tourist destination, Egypt. In 1972, they set up an investment agency, with the purpose of encouraging the creation of small and medium-sized enterprises with private funds. The state continued to be involved in the big sectors, but even there it gradually worked its way out. After 1987, efforts were made to reverse the situation so that the private sector would gradually become dominant and the public sector would systematically be drawn down. At the time that we spoke, the balance was 50-50 public-private, but the state was being systematically diminished, as the government focused on a constant and relentless upgrading of people and institutions.

And as for the schools, that year, they had 90 university level institutions and were building ten more. Every Tunisian child was in school, and God help the father or mother who even dared to think of not sending their children!

It must be remembered that all this had to be started literally from scratch. When the French went, they left nothing behind, and so the state had to step in. Even in the beginning, Bourguiba's Tunisia had not actually chosen state control; rather, it was from sheer necessity, when virtually all the French entrepreneurs were fleeing back to the continent and agriculture nearly collapsed from the disastrous first five years of fashionable collectivisation.

Economists divide 'New Tunisia's' economy into four cycles: the liberation of the country from the former colonial power, with all those experiments and mistakes; Ben Salah's efforts to turn Tunisia into a state of Yugoslav cooperatives; the 1970s when the country turned to liberalism and strong economic growth, and finally the Ben Ali period when the country forged ahead, liberalising and reforming its economy at every turn. Tunisia had put itself into a race with its capacities that was both exhilarating and exhausting – and, of course, imperfect – and yet Europe was happy about this, too. In the late 1980s when Bourguiba left office, Tunisian immigrants were swamping Europe. By 1999, there was virtually no emigration at all and most of the earlier immigrants had come home, except of course the fundamentalists who were definitely not welcome home again.

I then asked M. Merdassi the question I had asked almost everybody I talked to in Tunisia: 'Where did the ideas come from?' I had visited 120 countries in every corner of the globe, and what fascinated me always was that question of who had thought it all up. What did he and – one would always include in Tunisia, she – draw upon? Were there other examples that they had studied and adapted?

He paused thoughtfully before he answered. 'It's in the international air,' he replied. 'The ideas come from perhaps two or three blocs: Asia, the United States, Europe. Since about 1990, all the developing countries are moving the same way. Even China has chosen liberalisation. All your developing countries are seeking competitiveness. You have to make partners with your neighbours.' He paused and smiled. 'The world now,' he added, in what seemed to me to be an odd tone, 'is very small.'

I thought for a moment about the paradox. Actually, in the cold, unforgiving light of day, Tunisia was very small and the world was very big. But because the Tunisians had generally focused upon and chosen the right mix of ideas and the right evolutionary timing of the application of those ideas, the world now seemed very small to them and, in turn, the Tunisian experience seemed rather big to the world. I had a kaleidoscope once, and it taught me how forms and lights and shadows, circles and squares and bold lines, can be forced to form, and reform, and sparkle with difference, simply by turning the fascinating little 'machine'.

Tunisia's changes were infinitely more real, of course, than the shimmering images filtering through the kaleidoscope, and yet I had the feeling that one might somehow compare the two experiences.

A Thoughtful Walk Across Town

This particular late afternoon, as I often did when I was visiting in Tunisia, I decided to stop to see my colleague, Oussama Romdhani, the head of the Tunisian External Communications Agency, whose offices were housed in a typically unassuming, neat building in downtown Tunis just off Boulevard Bourguiba.

Earlier in the day, *en route* to one of my interviews, my driver took me through the new commercial and entertainment complex, *Les Berges du Lac* or the 'Shores of the Lake' along El Bouheyra, Lake Tunis. A flat salt lake like so many in north-eastern Tunisia, and the reason why so many travellers across the decades would praise the capital city as 'Green Tunis', this lake was for many years totally polluted. Today, the *Les Berges* development sits aside a sparkling body of water. It is a large development of banks, bowling alleys, canoe clubs, restaurants of every sort and a properly-bricked English promenade along the seaside for walkers. There is a 'Miami Skateboards' shop, a 'Carthage Amusement Park' and an 'Africana' store. Much of the world, even when it tries to do things like this, does them shabbily or cheaply, including in my own country. But I could not help thinking what an architecturally and artistically beautiful development this was, with its bright signs and charming yellow and white striped awnings. Somehow everything fitted, and one could even swim in the lake, edged by eucalyptus, palm, pine and oak trees.

As I watched the busy middle class families enjoying this new development, I thought to myself, 'This is what the modern Arab world could be!'

On the last part of my journey that day, I strolled across Casbah Square, the beautiful white and blue square that is really the centre of public and official Tunis. Then I walked through the medina, noticing with pleasure the exquisite hammered wooden doors with their lovely metal decorations, the tiled courts that one could peep into and the Andalusian-style black and white stripes boldly proclaiming everywhere: 'I am a doorway from Spain!' I stopped briefly in one of those mellow old cafés of the medina, with their deliciously shadowy entrances, and sipped a hot, thick black Turkish coffee. I found cybercafés right next door to these old places, while even in the medina many of the buildings had satellite dishes to enable them to get London Arab networks, the BBC and CNN and even, until 9/11 when it was taken off the air, the unwelcome Tunisian Islamist broadcasts from England. I peeked again into the Zeitouna mosque, to steep myself further in that special history, and I gazed at the ancient calendar in the central square of the mosque. For some reason, it seemed to me to be rather like an indicator of the past than of the future. It was sometimes hard to tell exactly where I was, because I was existing within a world of so much movement.

By the time I came to Avenue Bourguiba, close to the Information Bureau, I was enjoying the new sweep of refurbishment that seemed to have opened up the entire boulevard. When I first came in 1992, it had been a somewhat shabby old French colonial boulevard, with a tree-lined promenade down the centre and elegant, but scabrous, fronts to the mansions. A few modern hotels broke the low skyline. At the end of the street, a famous old train, built by the French, still carries people along most of the northern coast of the country. Now, too, thanks to still another typical Tunisian group, part government and part private, called the 'National Agency for the Preservation of the Medina', the old city had been beautifully cleaned up, and every front on Avenue Bourguiba was elegantly refurbished or completely redone in original style.

It happened to be a Friday morning, the Islamic sabbath. In virtually all of the rest of the Arab world, that would have meant, 'Forget the demands of globalisation and of being part of the larger economic world, this is the day you do not work!' But not here. With his attention to balance and his care for rational solutions, Bourguiba had arranged for Tunisians to work on Friday morning and Saturday morning and have Friday afternoon and all day Sunday off, thus observing the Islamic heritage but, as with all things here, modernising it and allowing Tunisians to compete in the world. Jewish holidays in Tunisia incidentally, are government-assured holidays for Tunisian Jews.

Finally, I paused in the central promenade, where four schoolgirls, probably nine or ten years of age, were practicing their English lessons like charming young magpipes. The two languages of Tunisia were Arabic and French, but I knew that after The Change all children had to learn English in school.

Once in his office, Oussama and I discussed what economist Merdassi had outlined for me. 'Yes...' Oussama said with some passion, 'What is the most important thing that has happened in the last ten years? The reinvention of hope! It used to be hard to come by. The country was very vulnerable; it was small, with no resources, and in France in those days, some foreign policy analysts, as those with *Le Monde*, used to speculate regularly about "When will Tunisia collapse?" Now, the young look at the future as within their grasp. The country is on the brink of a terrific victory. It was pulled from the brink, thanks to a few good men and women.'

What this meant personally in the life of one Tunisian man came across to me most forcibly the next afternoon when I was talking to an editor in the offices of the prominent Tunisian newspaper, *Le Temps*. We were discussing the difference on a personal level between the static, turgid, limiting old state control versus the new dynamism of the private sector being 'refereed' by the state. He pointed out to me the difference in employment philosophy and practices between the old centralised government, which controlled everything even remotely economic, and today's loosely planned and regulated free enterprise system. 'Before, the government employed all the engineers,' he said. 'I came back with a PhD as a civil engineer from Paris, where I had been working on the landing gear of the Concorde. I was told by the government to sit down and "wait till we tell you where to work." Then they put me in a totally administrative position. Today, thank God, all of that waste is over, and employment comes only through the firms.'

Under the rigid, unbending old system, Tunisians, like all North Africans, were pouring north to Italy, to Spain, to France, anywhere they could find work and hope and modernity. Now they are all coming 'home'. Tunisia had reversed yet another tenet of Third Worldism. Instead of a 'brain drain' from Tunisia to Europe, impoverishing the sender nation of its finest sons and daughters and enriching the receiving nation, Tunisians like this man, educated and trained in Europe, were coming back in a 'brain return'.

But Was it Really an Election?

The year 1999 was also the first time in Tunisian history that the country had multi-party elections – for parliament but also for president. 'For the first time – absolutely for the first time – we will have more than one candidate for president,' Minister Abdewahab Abdallah, the President's sophisticated spokesman, mused with me. 'Part of his overall strategy is to build a well-anchored democracy. We have entered a new stage in which the opposition will be enlarged. President Ben Ali's stage is "gradualism", and now we are entering a new stage in which the economic and social development will be accompanied by a political evolution. It's unavoidable, the rule of democracy in the world today.'

In short, another piece of the evolving mosaic was being put into place. In a very real sense, Tunisia was developing incipient democracy, or evolutionary democracy, or tutelary democracy, or authoritarian democracy, or guided democracy, all of which it has been called at various times, through becoming a kind of debating society. In Tunisia's unique and interesting system, ideas bubble up. They are discussed in trade unions, in schools and universities, in the sophisticated strategic thinking institutes. There are dialogues with youth, one involving 10,000 young people. There is a National Thinktank of Ideas and a Permanent Reflection Group. All of this is pragmatic and rational and, as they all stress, 'not doctrinaire' and it is in these areas, too, that one finds the real other elections.

The elections of 1999 were not perfect. There were seven parties, including the six opposition parties that ranged from fronts for some of the old Communists, to Libyan Arab nationalists, to Ba'athists of the pro-Iraqi strain (the Communists, as well as the Islamists, were banned) to one party that wanted to nationalise everything it saw. But no-one questioned for a moment that the ruling party of Bourguiba and Ben Ali, by this time having passed in name from the Destour Party to the Democratic Constitutional Rally, would win. There were still many obstacles in the way of an opposition victory, many of them not only procedural or public policy, but psychological. Until now, the voting results had been essentially foreordained by the candidate eligibility rules, which allowed only old has-beens to run against Ben Ali. As one foreign election observer noted, 'Anyone in his right mind would have voted for Ben Ali faced with this limited choice. Besides, genuine small 'd' democrats are few and far between in Tunisia.'

The ruling party seemed just too entrenched, too historic, too successful; Tunisia remained a one-party state and there were many people who had a solid interest in keeping it that way. And yet it was already changing. In that election, new and serious opposition candidates were accepted for the first time, most notably Mustapha Ben Jaafar, who heads what is acknowledged to be the most serious of the opposition parties. Ben Jaafar's candidacy shows that, at least to a degree, President Ben Ali's gradual movement towards multi-party democracy is beginning to take hold.

Both Bourguiba and Ben Ali had always feared making political changes too quickly, because too-rapid change could mean a loss of momentum in the economy and in the psychological development of the people. But now at least, the Ben Ali school of thinking within the party was ready to begin seriously to build democracy into all of the institutions of the nation. It sounded strange to the West, but the process was such that opposition parties were guaranteed 20 percent of the seats in the parliament, and for the most part were provided reasonably equal TV and newspaper coverage. The government provided them with subsidies for newsprint to advertise their policies, and debates occurred freely across the country. A law passed as early as 1997 had made it possible for every party to obtain an annual grant of approximately $60,000 to help it cover operating expenses, plus another grant of $5,000 payable to each party for every member representing them in parliament. The leaders of two out of the six opposition parties would run for office, and the government pledged that the 15-day election campaign would be totally open and free, while respectable foreign election observers were invited to observe the process.

Ben Ali understood the complications of this delicate moment. 'Ben Ali has frequently studied the problems inherent in the transition from a single to a multi-party system,' the President's advisor, Sadok Chaabane has written. 'He is perfectly aware of the fact that three decades have embedded the one party system into Tunisia's political life, and that any elimination of its consequences demands time and effort.' Ben Ali himself told me that one must 'take into consideration what I believe to be two essential factors, the young nature of the opposition parties on the one hand, and on the other, the long-standing experience of the ruling Democratic Constitutional Rally as well as its historic legitimacy, its wide influence and the major role it played in gaining independence and in building the modern state.'

Laying the foundations for democracy had taken decades in other countries, he went on, 'but we in Tunisia are trying to shorten the time period... adopting for this purpose formulas and incentives that are philosophically comparable to the approach of "affirmative action" in the American political and social experience.'

In the end, Ben Ali won 99 percent of the votes and his governing party, with 2.8 million votes, kept a strong lead which allowed it to earn 148 of the 182 seats of the seats in Parliament. But the opposition parties and the ten independent slates which took part in the legislative race garnered many more votes than in previous elections, earning, according to election figures, approximately 160,000 of the popular votes against only 64,000 in 1994. The opposition Social Democratic Movement came ahead of the rest of the opposition and a long 'out' party, the Liberal Social Party, entered Parliament for the first time, increasing the number of opposition parties within the chamber from four to five. This was exactly the kind of evolution that the governing forces had wanted.

The European Left scorned the results, of course, yet Western election observers told me that they had found a generally fair election. It should also be noted that Ben Ali did not have to call for elections at all – there were no laws, nor regulations, demanding it.

His supporters said that the government's popularity was such that he would have won anyway.

One journalist argued, 'Ben Ali's trying to give power away, but he has to find people who are willing to ask for power and credible enough to deserve it.' Then this man pointed to the example of Olusegun Obasanjo in Nigeria. He was arguably the best president and leader that this blighted and benighted country had had; but he left office voluntarily, before his work of transition was completed. He was arrested by the horrible dictatorship that succeeded him and finally came back to power in the 1990s. But now he took power hopelessly in a destroyed country. He could do virtually nothing for his ravaged country, torn by a bitter civil war between the Muslim North and the Christian South. 'Look at Obasanjo in Nigeria,' he said. 'Now he's being sworn in again, but this time he has nothing behind him and the country is close to civil war. All we ask is, please, put the picture into historical perspective and into geographical perspective. Are we better today than last year? The President told us his intention to hold elections and to move us forward – and now he's done it.'

'Our intention is to conciliate several concerns,' Mohamed Ghannouchi, the minister in charge of external economic affairs and later Prime Minister, told me. 'We aim for social progress through improving social conditions and democracy. Through these, gradually we create a new condition.'

'Ben Ali's not saying we're living in paradise,' one newspaper editor told me, 'he's just saying we're doing our best.'

When the Domestic Becomes the Foreign

It was Tunisia which took in the hostile Arab League after it split apart in Cairo following Egyptian President Anwar Sadat's trip to Jerusalem in 1978, a trip that was deeply unpopular in the Arab world. It was Tunisia which not only took in the Palestine Liberation Organisation in 1982, but then for the next 12 years endured all the problems of having these quixotic and dangerous guerrilla fighters in its midst. Arafat liked to change quarters every night, and the Israelis liked to bomb Tunis in order to kill PLO leaders. In fact, it was the PLO's Tunisian exile which caused it to moderate its stance so that it was willing to accept the Oslo Accords in 1993. It was Tunisia which was for many years a prime recipient of American aid, and who used it well for nearly three decades; Tunisia which was the first Arab and Muslim country to be genuinely open to joint business ventures so that they could finish the unfinished symphony of the Middle East; Tunisia which worked for peace in the Balkans and sent peacekeeping troops and field hospitals to that area and also to Afghanistan. The one place where Tunisia broke with the more progressive policies of the world was during the Gulf War against Iraq in 1991; it did not support the war, and did not take part in it, because of inter-Arab rivalries and feelings within its own borders. Washington never quite forgave Tunisia for this unexpected fall from grace.

The factor that many have missed in observing and analysing countries in transition like Tunisia or, in earlier years, Taiwan, Oman and Singapore, is that what countries like these have done on a national level, they have also done on the international level. The moderate, evolutionary, gradualist policies of Tunisia, both under President Bourguiba and President Ben Ali, were direct reflections of their policies at home. Interestingly enough, their domestic approach has had direct consequences in foreign policy. It is no accident that all of these small countries have internationally pushed for negotiation, mediation and justice; that they have worked for effective regional and international institutionalisation and that they have done far more than their share in peacekeeping and peace-enforcing.

All of this is hardly accidental, of course, because just as European and American foreign policies at their best were reflective of the internal principles of their democracies, so were Tunisia's. One could certainly argue that, if one wants a world community with common, constructive, creative diplomacy and a wise use of power, one should encourage these models of development internally in order to benefit from their reflection externally.

But What About Human Rights?
Virtually no-one in Tunisia today will deny that there have been human rights abuses over the years. Not even the President, nor most of the ruling party, will deny it. And surely not the Minister of Defence, an amenable, scholarly-looking lawyer named Dali Jazi. As

I sat talking with him one morning in the spring of 2002 in his elegant office, he calmly outlined those human rights abuses for me. His demeanor was quiet and thoughtful, but somehow I felt a great well of emotion in him, even though he spoke in a very modulated voice.

'Before 1987, we had no assurance that judicial custody did not exist,' he began soberly. 'The police could arrest and keep you in custody for an undetermined period of time. People talked about torture. In addition to that, a judge could keep custody and you could wait years and years before your case was brought before the court. But after 1987, the President changed the laws. Now there were two guarantees: one, that the period of custody be reduced to six days, and two, that with the constitutional reform adopted by parliament and passed by a popular referendum, guarantees of human rights have become part of the constitution. Human rights have been progressing for the last 14 years and that progress, of course, has been taking place in stages, consolidating human rights in harmony with economic development as the social level of Tunisia improved and as freedom for women developed.'

At this point, I found myself becoming interested as to why a minister of defence, whose primary job, after all, was the direction and overseeing of the Tunisian military, should be so interested in human rights, in law and in questions of retribution and justice. Why, indeed? But before we could get to those questions, we talked about the army. The Tunisian army had three essential missions, he carefully explained to me.

First, there was the classic mission of protecting the security of the nation and of securing the frontiers: we know that Tunisia had plenty of trouble with its frontiers, with Muammar Khadafy's belligerent, terrorist-training Libya on one side and civil war-torn Algeria on the other. Tunisia might have a small army, but it was serious. It had kibbutz-style missions, which were military but also economic, on Tunisia's border with Algeria, where fundamentalist groups were still waging a brutish war, cutting the throats of hundreds of villagers every day. 'It has not always been easy with neighbours who were not very wise but with whom we maintain a good understanding,' he said carefully. Secondly, the military also contributed to the well-being of the country, and this included taking part in the constant fight against desertification, planting palm trees in the South, helping nomads to settle in palm groves, improving social programmes, building bridges and houses, aiding in natural calamities and building roads. I would have liked to ask him if the army had built our road with the white line through it in the South, but he continued talking, and the moment passed.

The third was the international dimension: Tunisia has become known for its willingness and spirit with regard to peacekeeping tasks of the world. The Tunisian military has had officers in Congo, Rwanda, Burundi, Somalia and Bosnia. They sent a hospital to Afghanistan and provided other public works and aid to Kosovo.

It was not lost on me, although it saddened me to think of it, that Tunisia was now sending peacekeepers to all those countries which had taken the Third World way, or the Marxist way, or simply your generic African, brutal 'Big Man' dictator way after decolonisation. Tunisia, which had gone its own way, was being forced to minister to the expensive failures of countries which had so highhandedly refused to create those Tunisian-style 'antibodies' against violence and chaos.

I was still curious as to why the Defence Minister, not the Education Minister, not the Social Welfare Minister, not the Minister of Women's Affairs, should be talking so knowledgeably, and with such obvious concern, about human rights. Then he explained it to me.

'I was a professor of constitutional law at the university from 1992 to 1999,' he said. 'I am a professor of constitutional law. I taught in the United States and England. I understand modern multi-party democracy and I understand Montesquieu. Then I became the Minister of Higher Education. But I was an activist in human rights work from 1976 onwards. I was one of the principle founders of the Tunisian League of Human Rights, the first in the Arab and African world. Actually, I was in the democratic opposition during President Bourguiba's presidency.' He paused. 'I was never avid for power,' he continued, 'and I am not a professional politician. In fact, I was a member of the opposition. I only did what I could for the democratic opposition. Then I became part of Ben Ali's team in 1989. I worked for human rights in the capacity of the Ministry of Health.' He smiled. 'And today I have landed here.'

In those early years, he defended many people, he said, most often against the government. 'For 19 years, I pleaded for justice for many,' he went on. 'I defended them against arbitrary arrests, against torture and for the right to self expression. But as soon as I had to deal with a group that resorted to violence – no!'

His time as a lawyer had coincided with those years when Communism and fundamentalism were working against the government, and I asked him whether he had ever defended a fundamentalist.

'Sincerely, no,' he answered, 'for I only defend those who themselves defend democratic rights. I never defended a terrorist because I consider myself a democrat. If I'd been a German or a Pole in 1936, I couldn't have defended a Nazi against a Jew. I defend the true definition of freedom. For the rest, I trust the justice of the courts.'

I realised that I had come upon one of the keys to the Tunisian experience. In the purist Western sense of human rights, which arose incrementally out of the Western experience and was rooted in Anglo-Saxon jurisprudence, the case study system and the natural rights of man, many Western lawyers would feel self-righteous about defending absolutely anyone. Indeed, there was often a certain pride in taking on the worst murderer, the most vicious Communist or Nazi, a rapist of children or a violator of the innocents. Among certain legal élites in the West, this was considered a way of making you more morally and professionally 'pure'. This attitude was joined, in the spirit of the Third World, but also the Communist world, by new statements and supposed processes, like the U.N. Universal Declaration of Human Rights, which soberly spelled out every possible right that every single human being in every possible corner of the world must have.

But this was falsity of a most cruel kind, for none of these putative 'rights' could or would ever be actually applied, for there was no way to implement them, no way to enforce them and no depth in most of these societies for their people even to know of them. In this way of thinking, law did not need to become reality, it only needed to be proclaimed. This was the Third World dilemma and the Third World sickness. What it ultimately did was to set back work on human rights all over the world, because when such declarations did not automatically ensure human rights and human development, the hope for them and the effort put behind them would fade.

From the very beginning, Tunisia did not believe it could afford false promises or such rhetoric, all proclaimed so self-righteously at the expense of reality.

Dali Jazi perfectly characterised the Tunisian approach. 'I think it would be a mistake to say that we grant all the rights theoretically only to find that people couldn't apply them,' he said slowly and thoughtfully. 'There are things that are clear to the life of a people, and there is an intimate harmony which must coexist with the progress of the people.'

But then he added, 'That does not stop us from saying that there are fundamental rights that must be protected, for everybody and by everybody. I speak of inhuman treatment, degrading torture, arbitrary arrest, any type of violence and any religious intolerance. Because freedom of expression cannot exist unless a true sense of moderation lives within everybody.'

Every once in a while in Tunisia, thoughtful people will carefully compare Tunisia's evolutionary approach – based upon principle, not theory – to the experience of the United States, and this is accurate. But the West had both space and time, whereas after independence, Tunisia didn't have either. It had to propound, form and bring to fruition all of these changes virtually overnight, in a small and threatened piece of land, essentially during the life of one generation.

'When, during the revolution in the US, you established your Constitution in 1787 and proclaimed the equal rights of all citizens, it still took a lot of time for racial equality to evolve,' Dali Jazi went on. 'You needed people like John F. Kennedy and Martin Luther King Jr. A text is always generational and it needs a certain time for the political culture to allow for the full acceptance of the law. Ben Ali, for instance, borrows elements from many areas. International pacts, civilian and political rights, economic, cultural and social rights. He took human rights principles from international instruments, and the next reform will mean integrating them into the constitution to give them more of a legal structure.'

Meanwhile, the outcry against Tunisia's internal human rights violations continued unabated from Europe. From London, Rached Ghannouchi, the long-time leader of the Islamists in Tunisia, was now broadcasting on radio and TV to his homeland. In exile, An Nahda was still demanding that women be put under the veil and that Tunisia be brought under the strict Muslim shar'ia law, on the model of the Ayatollah Khomeini's retrogressive state in Iran in the 1980s. He was glorifying the martyrdom of the Al Qaeda terrorists. His group had started a *Zeitouna* TV channel, giving it the same name as the university and the mosque, because 'Zeitouna is our heritage'. Of course, it no longer was, if indeed it really ever had been.

Meanwhile, the Tunisian government from time to time brought men and women to trial for various common law offences, despite the fact that these people were often only foolish, theatrical or thoroughly unimportant dissidents. This only gave fuel to the European Left and to the exiled Islamists' arguments. All of this was made possible by the European, and in particular the British, policies of political asylum; purist policies that would soon come under grave attack after the terrorist attacks of 9/11 and the realisation on the part of many European governments that they had actually been harbouring, not genuine political refugees, but something quite different.

Many liberal-minded and loyal Tunisians have spoken repeatedly with the President and with officials about these trials, arguing that they accomplish very little except turning foreign public opinion against Tunisia. But they continue, in large part apparently because of the Tunisian idea that the leader must never show weakness, particularly against a subversive dissent. Meanwhile, the Tunisian lawyers for the dissidents have often become *cause célèbres* in Europe, whose openness and freedom they cynically use to call the Muslim world back to its most retrogessive self.

As for the President, he sustains no doubts about his actions. 'Let me be clear about the fact that there are no political prisoners in Tunisia,' Ben Ali told me in 1998. 'All those in prison in Tunisia are there for common law crimes. They have been judged by the ordinary courts, in accordance with ordinary procedures, and in application of the law and have been found guilty of established actions involving, in most cases, terrorism or aggravated violence, or related to the preparation of acts of violence directed at overthrowing the republican regime. Those who respect the law in Tunisia are not disturbed, as we live here under the rule of law.'

A New Legitimacy

By the spring of 2002, still more changes were in the air, changes which they said would move the country far beyond all those old human rights problems of the past.

In his message to the nation on November 7, 2001, which was the 14th anniversary of The Change, President Ben Ali announced his intention to introduce a major constitutional reform project that will 'enable us to make a quantum leap in our political system...' Human rights and liberties, including such everyday but crucially important rights as freedom from preventive custody and procedures related to police custody and to preventive detention, would be written into the constitution. Tunisia would become one of the first countries worldwide to show interest in the 'fourth-generation of human rights,' which included the question of bio-genetic ethics, scientific experiments and communications technologies. These were now to be enshrined in the constitution. A two-chamber system of government was to be instituted, composed mostly of elected members but also including professional businessmen and representatives from the regions and provinces. It would also include certain aspects of the parliamentary system, such as the vote-of-no-confidence and written and oral question sessions.

As with the last plan, it contained myriad small reforms that would move the country forward and give individuals more power. A reduction of tariffs in data transmission networks intended for economic enterprises; an increase in the capacity of the digital phone network; an in-depth study of the phenomenon of climatic changes and its impact upon the agricultural sector and the eco-system; a call to regional development boards to support private investment; a doubling of the capital of investment companies in the north-west, mid-west and south; a reinforcement of the forms of dialogue in the written press, on radio and television, including a television programme for the first time to provide live coverage of parts of the Chamber of Deputies; and an 'intelligence economy in a society of knowledge'.

And then a growing consolidation of pluralism in public life; protecting the right to privacy; starting two science and technology centres in Borj Cedria and Sidi Thabet; a strategic study on handicrafts by the year 2016; the establishment of the World Solidarity Fund and the creation of an International Prize for Islamic Studies to be awarded by the President of the Republic to moderate Muslim thinkers, with the purpose of enriching the interpretative thinking based on dialogue and openness.

When Ben Ali spoke that day at Carthage Palace, the panorama of accomplishment which he laid out was profoundly impressive. Life expectancy at birth was now 73 years and would exceed 74 years by 2006. The schooling rate was currently over 99 percent for six-year old boys and girls and the rate of enrolment in higher education was over 28 percent for the 20 to 24 age group. It was expected to exceed 35 percent in 2006 and 40 percent by 2010, against six percent in 1987. Since The Change, the number of university students had doubled nearly seven times over, and the number of subjects, in new universities that were bursting forth all over the country, had increased from 200 to 400. The number of university students was estimated to reach 350,000 in two years from now and more than 500,000 before 2010.

But there was one highly controversial part of this new plan which made many even sympathetic observers of the Tunisian model hold their breath. In 1987, one of the first things that Zine El Abidine Ben Ali had done was to abolish Bourguiba's beloved and self-established title of 'President-for-Life'. Now President Ben Ali was himself overseeing the removal of the prohibition on term limitations which would have seen him out of office after three five-year terms, forcing him to retire in 2004. There would still however, be the age limit of 75. Ben Ali has also pledged to hold free and fair elections and facilitate rival candidacies to the office of President.

The Tunisian process was not yet finished, officials explained, and after all, the country remained in the throes of the promising, but at the same time dangerous, transition to European integration. 'Let him finish the transition which he started when the country fully joins the developing world and is a fully democratised country,' they said. And they were beginning to call the system 'presidential democracy'.

In the end, then, one can picture the country gradually moving to a new, truly multi-party stage, with perhaps today's ruling party transforming itself gradually into a competitive party. One can imagine in Tunisia something approximating the model of Europe, with its tendency to place more conservative Christian Democrat (and thus, loosely religious) parties up against more liberal and secular Social Democratic ones. One can also picture a party that does not say it is Islamic, because that would be illegal, but a party that draws more fully upon Islamic awareness and principles, one perhaps formed in the image of the Turkish Islamic Party model.

It all depends ultimately upon what Zine El Abidine Ben Ali does in the next ten years, upon what the new generation of leadership, the excellent younger governors of the regions, who are now in their 40s and 50s, really have in their hearts and souls, and upon how outside forces, in particular the world economy, globalisation and potential wars in the Middle East, play into the Tunisian equation.

But others worried, at least for the moment, about the imbalance of economic and social development, which was superb, as against political development, which was still not completely formed. Typical was the thinking of one Western diplomat in Tunis, who told me, 'The worry now is whether Ben Ali can keep up with the need for political change. We hope he is wise enough to use his accomplishments and leave this as a legacy. The opposition is hopeless, but there should at least be an orderly succession within the party. But if the economy were to slip really badly, the country could see a rebirth of fundamentalism.' Then he said thoughtfully, 'The next hurdle is on the political side, but still... Tunisia does have the chance to be the first modern Arab nation.'

The Country that Works
In the meantime, the Tunisians seem to have arrived at a truly workable and appropriate formula, which they are daily putting bravely into practice against all the chaos and absolutism swirling

about them in the world. Importantly for such a highly non-ideological and anti-absolutist experiment, where catchy and emotional slogans do not roll easily off the tongue, still they know what they are doing and they know how to characterise what they are doing. 'Once people get busy working, and dreaming, the grip of old values that are not congenial to modern life begins to fade,' was the way one leading official put it. 'It all goes back to one basic concept,' Minister Abdewahab Abdallah, the softly-spoken, worldly spokesman for the Presidency, told me one day, 'and that is an equal chance at life. There are no glass ceilings here, regional and gender mobility is almost limitless and this reality reinforces the large middle class, because opportunities are so accessible.'

It was Abdelbaki Hermassi however, who put the experiment in the most elegant, enlightening terms. 'In this kind of post-ideological period, people rely on their instincts, and they will judge their leadership on the life chances it provides for them,' he told me. That same day, as I wandered through the medina I thought about the old legitimacies that I had myself as a journalist witnessed in the world – everything from the God-given right of kings, the familiar and tribal authority of sultans, emirs and sheikhs, the spell of charismatic leadership, the violent takeover of the soul by the Islamic fundamentalists, the words of Karl Marx, the thrill of unbridled nationalism and finally the new attraction of types of representative and democratic government, paired with economic freedom and civil participation. Gradually I realised that what I was seeing worked out and exemplified in Tunisia was really a new form of legitimacy.

'Ideology is dead,' Abdelbaki Hermassi had once said to me thoughtfully as we discussed his country. 'What we now have here is a new legitimacy, based on the actual achievement of results for the people.'

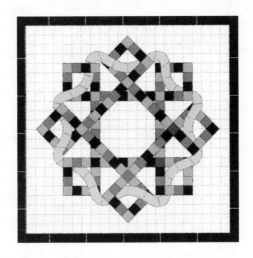

7. Tunisia, One Mosaic: *Islands of Prosperity and Progress in a Sea of Poverty and Chaos*

'The tortoise countries have won the race.'

Joseph Stiglitz, winner of the Nobel Memorial Prize for Economics

Tunisia After 9/11

When I returned to Tunisia in the spring of 2002, the world had been turned upside down. The United States had been traumatised, as never before in its history, by the Middle Eastern terrorist attacks of September 11, 2001. Europe was in the process of trying to transform its historic borderlands from Turkey to Eastern Europe, and now Tunisia, through the economic reforms of the European Union. But terrorism was affecting that vast mission, as well as poisoning so much else in the world. From most of the other nations of North Africa, emigrants still poured out to make the short, life-transforming trip to Europe. Governments were being overwhelmed by desperate immigrants all too willing to face the perilous crossing for a share in the civilised life.

Tunisia was one of only a handful of small countries in the world that was continuing to forge ahead for all of its citizens, in part because it had got rid of its own Islamist radical movements well before they could totally threaten the state. Suddenly, the Tunisian experiment had even more importance for the world, for the whole vexed question of 'development' or 'nation-building' had once again risen to the surface of the mind of the world, this time in a profoundly dangerous manner.

With the war in Iraq, the United States joined the ranks of countries, governments and peoples who seemed to believe in the old magic of 'overnight development'. Iraq would become 'democratised' and 'reconfigured', its people throwing flowers at the feet of their Western 'liberators'. Old nuances once again threatened to become new traumas, as the old spontaneous combustion form of development threatened once again to overshadow and even to overcome the Tunisian way of evolutionary development in harmony with human nature and human culture.

Even more importantly, one could see that what was coming across the entire world was more disintegration and more violent breakdown. The future would turn, even more than before, on whether systems and structures could be formed and nurtured in poor countries that give people control over their own lives. But Tunisia also stood as an example of how to modernise, not against the West as so many Arab countries had tried to do, but with the West, while at the same time maintaining its own dignity and culture.

Once again, Tunisia itself was reminded savagely of its old trauma when, in the spring of 2002, one of the old Tunisian Islamists, by then long exiled in Germany, blew up his truck outside the legendary synagogue on the island of Djerba, killing innocent German tourists who had stopped there for only a few moments to admire the building. The attack was clearly an outcome and an overflow of the Al Qaeda attacks across the world; but what was so different about Tunisia, once again, was the fact that the Tunisian police immediately uncovered the European-based plot, that there was an outpouring of sympathy for both Jews and Germans on the part of the Tunisian people, and that such an attack, in Tunisia, had become so very out of date and out of order.

I thought as I arrived that April day in 2002 that Tunisians could have been forgiven for taking the attitude, 'We told you so.' But far from being smug, or even pleased that they had been right, the Tunisians I spoke to were saddened by the outcome of so many years of struggle. As for myself, I felt that a great part of their sadness was to be found in the hard-won realisation that it could all have been so different. They were, after all, the living proof of that.

This time, I found Habib Ben Yahia in the new Foreign Ministry building just outside the medina. His old office had been in an exquisite, intricately decorated jewel-box of a room in one of the finest old beylical palaces. The new building, modern and also beautiful, took its style from the old palace, but it was infinitely more comfortable and more workable. It was so typical of Tunisia, I thought. Once again I was finding progress without disruption, infused with a harmonious flow of the nation's culture and a movement into the future, all carefully calibrated so that there was no opportunity for a disrupting denial of the past.

'We had been telling Washington for years that Afghanistan was a nest of terrorists,' Habib Ben Yahia said, as we sat drinking Tunisian tea in his beautiful new office (he still missed the old one, he admitted). 'Since the 1980s, we kept telling the West that we've got to take care of Afghanistan, with its mixture of terrorism, Islam and drugs. We made it known to the Americans and to the Europeans that the wound had been left open. But Afghanistan, and thus the roots of the terrorist problem, was on the back burner. We are not telling anyone "we told you so", but in fact, action should have been taken earlier.'

In Afghanistan, he went on, 'we not only need to reconstruct roads and bridges, but mentalities.' He paused. 'As Muslims, we have good experience, and modernising Afghanistan is more urgent than roads and bridges.' Then, reflecting on Tunisia's own dramatic experience of modernisation in the mid-19th century, he added, 'Remember that out of Afghanistan came the first Islamic reformers, late in the 19th century. Then the Soviets came in 1979 and the whole thing changed. What they need now is not a revolution but a resumption of that early Afghani – and Islamic – life.'

Then came the American invasion of Iraq, with all the questions it has raised about the quest for development and democratisation or, at least, for forms of representative government and for the influence of one country's system on another country's memory.

The New Thinking

That very same spring, there emerged across the world an entirely new school of thinking about development. I began to discover, often in supposedly disconnected countries and in minds formed by wholly different cultures, a welcome new realism about what it really takes to move a country and a people into the modern world.

First came the negative reinforcements to the Tunisian way, which highlighted the exhaustion with which many thinkers and activists were viewing the old ways of the purists of the past. In the late half of 2002, for instance, the United Nations Development Programme issued its annual report, *Human Development Report 2002: Deepening Democracy in a Fragmented World*. It reported that, although 81 countries had moved into the democratic column and some 33 military governments had been replaced by civilian governments since 1980, 'one multi-party election does not a democracy make.' In fact, 'the international cheerleaders for democracy have underestimated what it takes to build a functioning, properly rooted democracy,' the development programme's administrator Mark Malloch Brown said at the time. 'Democracy doesn't seem to be responding to the real agenda of the world's poor.' The report found that new democratic hopes unmet by elected governments too often led only to public disgust for the system and regression to military rule; it noted, for instance, the situation in Pakistan in 1999.

Fareed Zakaria, the brilliant young Pakistani thinker on foreign affairs, published an influential and thoughtful book entitled, *The Future of Freedom: Illiberal Democracy at Home and Abroad*, in which he stated forthrightly that, 'Democracy is flourishing; constitutional liberalism is not. Today 118 of the world's 193 countries are democratic, encompassing a majority of its people... In this season of victory, one might have expected Western statesmen and intellectuals to... give a rousing three cheers for democracy. Instead, there is a growing unease at the rapid spread of multi-party elections... perhaps because of what happens after the elections.' This is because, 'without a background in constitutional liberalism, the introduction of democracy in divided societies has actually fomented nationalism, ethnic conflict and even war.'

When the political system is opened up, diverse groups with incompatible interests gain access to power and press their demands. Political and military leaders, often embattled remnants of the old authoritarian order, realise that to succeed they must rally the masses behind a national cause. The result is invariably aggressive rhetoric and policies, which often drag countries into confrontation and war. The problems of governance in the 21st century, he summed up, are most likely to be problems within democracy. This makes them more difficult to handle, wrapped as they are in 'the mantle of legitimacy'.

Susan Woodward, a professor of political science at the City University of New York Graduate Centre, added to this debate, writing that, 'There's a large literature showing that, with democratisation, you're more likely to have violence.' Early elections strengthen people who are armed, like warlords, for they can use their weapons to confront opponents and intimidate voters.'

In his book *Race and Culture: A World View*, the African-American scholar Thomas Sowell also looked deeply into the cultural problem at the very heart of development questions. The respected professor rejected the current specious 'cultural relativism' arguments (all cultures are equivalent), and showed how in earlier times, and largely through conquest and empire, cultural traits travelled from one people to another, enlightening and advancing in turn (the far more efficient Arabic letters taking over from Roman numerals for example). But today's exaggerated cultural 'identity', he wrote, 'makes copying others akin to treason,' as 'lagging groups' are 'sealed off from the cultural advantages of the larger society around them.'

In fact, Sowell hit upon a crucially important point – one that is thoroughly un-politically correct, which is that if you are not willing to say that certain cultural values are superior to others and you are not willing to insist that countries adapt to them, those countries in need will simply never develop. Development is an ongoing lottery, a constant process of point and counter-point, with new syntheses constantly arising across history. German tribes were dancing naked around the fires of northern Europe when Egypt was at its height; ancient Cambodia was the centre of the south-eastern Asian cultural empires when Russians were living in wooden huts and struggling across the tundras in primitive sleds; and the ancient walls of Zimbabwe in Africa were being built when there was no America at all.

This was another secret of the Tunisian way: forget cultural jealousies, borrow what you need from other cultures that are more advanced in certain sectors, but, at the same time, love, cossett and preserve the jewels and strengths of your own culture, lest you lose yourself through being unable to digest change. The fine writer Bruce Chatwin called this, 'waiting for your souls to catch up.'

I was beginning to find bits and pieces in very varied places. One night I was having dinner in Washington with the Governor of Irkutsk, the historic city out in the middle of Siberia where, in earlier centuries, so many political exiles had been sent that this remote and seemingly isolated city always remained in the avant of the sluggish, rigid and cruel world of Soviet Communism. As this man pondered where Russia was going, he began to muse, 'Evolution... that is what works. Remember, the United States had years of evolutionary development. In America, the banks had many roles – social development, mortgages, savings. We never had that, we have to develop it.' And in the words of Marwan Muasher, the accomplished Foreign Minister of Jordan, 'Democracy is a cultural thing. It does not come with a syringe.'

Next, I came across some remarks of Eduard Shevardnadze, the elegant, silver-haired former Foreign Minister of the Soviet Union in the pivotal years of the 1980s. It was his ideas of *glasnost* and *perestroika* ('opening' and 'restructuring') that had transformed the Soviet Union and changed the world. But it was one thing to proclaim ideas, and quite another to put them into practice, taking into consideration the twists and turns of organisation and the vagaries of human nature. When Shevardnadze went back to his home in the Republic of Georgia, which after 1991, was an independent country, and became the country's first president, he found to his dismay how difficult it was to bring his ideas to reality. I had several interviews with him, and he said once with some despondence, 'Reform is not a revolution. Reform takes time. It requires a change in mentality or mind-set.'

Socialised Modernity

'We were not born into it,' Habib Ben Yahia had said to me during one of our talks. In fact, none of these 'new' countries were 'born into' modernity and the point was clear: America and most of the West had been able to develop naturally and organically, in linear manner, over centuries; these new countries needed to develop artificially, laterally and inorganically, over periods of years or even months. How unspeakably different – and how difficult!

But if not only Communism and absolutist political faiths had failed but also pure, overnight multi-party democracy and instant economic globalisation too – then what exactly was the answer?

Larry Diamond, the Stanford University democracy expert and one of the clearest thinkers on these subjects, said at the time of 9/11 that, 'there is no way out of the dilemmas of the Arab world without some political opening. But it doesn't start by holding elections now. What is needed is a managed political opening, coincident with economic reform, that can generate a middle class with respect for the rule of law and institutions. It requires a gradual process, with a vision from the top, that introduces pluralism into political life. The objective is to create a body for people who can one day contest for power in a responsible way, with the regimes keeping some reserve of power for themselves as insurance.'

It is difficult to find a better description of the Tunisian pattern than this. But perhaps the most brilliant and convincing words of all on this subject came from the economist Joseph Stiglitz, winner of the Nobel Memorial Prize in Economic Sciences. His original and innovative work was highly critical of international economic institutions like the World Bank and the International Monetary Fund, essentially because they usually strove for overnight development 'shock therapy' and rarely took into account Tunisian-style gradualism and integration of factors.

First he took on the questions of the purist globalisers who were arguing that the nation-state itself was an unnecessary anachronism and only part of the structural detritus of history, to be bypassed by a gauzy, vague new 'internationale' of international companies that worked the airwaves and the web and made nation-states a thing of the past. No! said Stiglitz, all wrong! No other basic entity of international life can replace the state, because the state is 'all we have as a means of ordering our international existence and of achieving representative government and protecting individual rights. In culture, economic success depends upon a certain amount of cohesion. Violence is one of the most adverse qualities to economic success. Culture is one of the glues for development.'

And so, said Joseph Stiglitz, the answer was 'gradualism'. Why? 'Because one of the most important aspects of change is to regulate the pace of change so people can adapt and create a strong culture. A slightly slower change will in the long run be faster. The tortoise countries have won the race.'

In short, in the end only a progressive nation-state truly stood between the comforting but restrictive world of the tribe and the anomie and lostness of the communised or globalised utopian world.

Sounding almost like the Tunisians, Joseph Stiglitz argued cogently that, 'Liberalising a country's trade makes sense when its industries have matured sufficiently to reach a competitive level, but not before. Privatising government-owned firms makes sense when adequate regulatory systems and corporate governance laws are in place, but not before.' Why, for instance, were there so many successful societal models in East Asia – Taiwan, Singapore, South Korea, as well as other models in the Persian Gulf, like the Sultanate of Oman and Bahrain, and Eastern European models like Slovenia and Poland?

'Here is the key distinction,' Stiglitz argued. 'Each of the most successful globalising countries determined its own pace of change, each made sure as it grew that the benefits were shared equitably. They were able substantially to control the terms on which they engaged with the global economy... The problem is not with globalisation but with how it has been managed.' Interestingly enough, and in contrast to the common fashionable mindset, he put the emphasis 'not on what developing countries have in common, but on how each is different.' This observation rang true, recalling again Habib Bourguiba's early 'specificity' of place and of culture, and Ben Ali's later adoption of the same principle, in place of Communism's 'internationalism' or Arab nationalism's bombastic ethnic egomania.

Some were giving this new form of the old 'enlightened autocracy' terms like 'progressive authoritarianism' or 'pragmatic gradualism'.

But far more important was Stiglitz' favourite term, 'sequencing', which simply meant not imagining that things could change overnight, but taking development steps one after the other.

In fact, the Nobel prize-winner's 'sequencing' was the blood-brother of reformer Habib Bourguiba's early 'gradualism' and of the Tunisian state's 'evolutionary development'.

Not Alone in the World

Even more astonishing for me was the discovery not only that Tunisia was 'making it' in the world, but that Tunisia was only one of an entire group of countries across the globe that was making it – and, most importantly, virtually all in the same way.

One of the primary models is that of Taiwan, the small and intrinsically poor island off the south-east coast of China. How could Taiwan, the place where the miserable and defeated Chinese nationalists came in 1949 after being defeated by the Chinese Communists, possibly have made it?

Firstly, it is a small island, only 242 miles from north to south and 87 miles from east to west, with two-thirds of its land mass high mountains or hills. In fact, it could be described as a mere rock, threatened always from outside by the Communists and threatened from within by the struggle between native Taiwanese and nationalist mainlander 'invaders'. And if you looked at the little island from the vantage point of resources, economics and political history, you could easily come to the conclusion that it was doomed. In fact, however, Taiwan would come to have a similar development psychology to Tunisia.

In 1997, I did some major research on the island. It was all-too clear that this, supposedly innocuous place had not only become a 'normal' country, despite the dramatic historic abnormality all around it, but that it had become a veritable model for the world. With only 21.4 million Taiwanese, as against 1.2 billion Chinese, Taiwan's per capita income was $13,000 and expected soon to be $20,000. Whereas mainland China had little of Confucianism left after half a century of Communism, Taiwan's businesspeople (and, of course, others) had respected the past. They were thriving on Confucian ethics and were therefore reliable international partners.

Taiwan was the world's 14th largest trading nation and the 17th largest economy, with reserves of $100 billion, second only to Japan's. 'If one were to look for one country in the world that has done everything right, that country would be Taiwan,' Lester Brown, one of the world's most prominent environmentalists, told me at the time. But why?

They left people on the land by locating factories in the countryside, investing almost totally in small and medium-sized industries (which were at that time 96 percent of all industries on the island). They encouraged private enterpreneurship at every turn. They invested so heavily in computer technology that, by the end of the 20th century, Taiwan was the third-largest producer of such technology in the world, after the United States and Japan. Finally, and the key to all success, they gradually but systematically adapted the earlier autocratic political system of General Chiang Kai-shek and his often corrupt but also clever and ultimately progressive cronies to today's democratic one. By the end of the 20th century, in contrast to its early days when the politics of the island were dominated by the nationalist Kuomintang Party, Taiwan had become a working democracy, with several parties, serious electoral debates and a populace that was more concerned with having fun with their children and fighting street crime than reviving the Middle Kingdom. The political changes were carefully thought-out and carefully orchestrated by the Kuomintang, which then swiftly began to lose elections and had to contend with the other parties, just like another party.

Yes, Taiwan had become 'normal', and it had actually become somewhat boring. There were no revolutions or rebellions anymore to make the blood flow, hardly even any demonstrations (except against street crime). And normal was perhaps the most difficult thing of all to be in a world of change and trauma.

Despite their real attempts to blend Confucianism with modernity, there was sometimes a sense of lostness and stress, because, as one top official told me, 'Taiwan has been industrialised so fast that people have lost their traditions, and yet the new norms have not yet been established.' For some, there was a gap in social norms. There was also the real chance, either that the powerful mainland would attack Taiwan, attempting to take it by force or – a reality that became ever more possible after the beginning of the 21st century – simply absorb its active and aggressive economics. Still, it was well worth the study.

Fareed Zakaria believes that the recent history of East Asia, with its highly successful pattern of development, has worked in great part because it has followed the Western itinerary. 'After brief flirtations with democracy after World War II, most East Asian regimes turned authoritarian,' he wrote. 'Over time, they moved from autocracy to liberalising autocracy, and, in some cases, toward liberalising semi-democracy. Most of the regimes in East Asia remain only semi-democratic, with patriarchs or one-party systems that make their elections ratifications of power rather than genuine contests.' But at the same time, 'These regimes have accorded their citizens a widening sphere of economic, civil, religious and limited political rights. As in the West, liberalisation in East Asia has included economic liberalisation, which is crucial in promoting both growth and liberal democracy...'

Zakaria is not the only accomplished analyst who traces the Western world's progress through just such similar journeys. He traces how, in 1215 at Runnymede, England's barons forced the king to abide by the settled and customary law of the land. In the American colonies these laws were made explicit, and in 1638 the town of Hartford adopted the first written constitution in modern history. In the 1970s, Western nations codified standards of behaviour for regimes across the globe. The Magna Carta, the Fundamental Orders of Connecticut, the American Constitution and the Helsinki Final Act are all expressions of constitutional liberalism.

In fact, think of Oman, South Korea, Singapore, Slovenia, Botswana, and Poland. All of these countries have made the difficult transition from the depths of impoverishment to true progress within one or, at the most, two generations of the modern age. Each one developed separately but, curiously enough, according to amazingly similar patterns. Serious men and women who came from different parts of the globe seemed to understand instinctively this new evolutionary ideology of timed growth, of gradual but persistent enlargement of the political sector and of the importance of cultural relatedness with the past for a true blossoming in the future.

I witnessed another example of gradualism or evolutionary development one day in 1995 in Oman, the small sultanate to the east of Saudi Arabia. Here you had a country that was at the very bottom of the development heap in 1970. That year, the old Sultan, who had kept his people in a state of penury in a country with just four schools and only a few miles of roads, was overthrown peacefully by his son, the young Sandhurst-trained Sultan Qaboos, in a bloodless coup. (For his part, the old Sultan died peacefully some years later living in a fashionable London hotel.) The young Sultan, devoted to his people and to his troubled country, immediately took action to quell a Marxist guerrilla movement in the southern province of Dhofar, over the border from Yemen, by making its leaders his own top ministers (just as Bourguiba had so often co-opted his enemies); then he put into practice a reasonable and evolutionary development model very similar to the Tunisian one.

That year, I went for one of my many interviews with the Sultan in his exquisitely decorated, but small and somehow reasonable, palace in Muscat. He had just opened Sultan Qaboos University and I knew of his dedication to women's education (a dedication not at all unknown in the uniquely progressive monarchies of the Arabian Gulf). So, of course, I asked him about women's studies there. This handsome man, with his arresting deep eyes and his fine Gulf robes, told me that even though people thought of him as an absolute monarch, he could not command the tribal leaders in Oman to obey his will, for these Gulf monarchies most definitely had representative government features built into them (like the Friday meetings between the people and the monarch, in which the monarch is bound to listen to the problems of his subjects face-to-face). No, he said, they would simply stay in their villages and fortified towns and set up roadblocks and defy him if, God forbid, he was to do something so foolish as to oblige their daughters to sit next to boys in the university.

So, he told me, with a pleased smile, he had devised a plan. He constructed the university complex with two walkways, one on the first floor, where the young male students would pass from their dormitories to their classrooms, and one on the second floor, where the young women students would pass from their dormitories to the same classrooms. Once there, the boys would sit on one side of the classroom and the girls on the other. It would not always be that way, he told me, but for the beginning that would work. And it did – and it has – and every year there is more 'give' in the process.

By the turn of the 21st century, there were more and more examples. In Oman, the vote was constantly being expanded; in Bahrain, the Emir was changing the system from an autocratic to a constitutional monarchy. In Slovenia, admittedly a different case because of its positioning in Europe, and yet still related, every small town had a factory to keep people in the villages rather than pouring helplessly (and violently) into the cities, one of the very major problems of the Third World. In Botswana, at least until the AIDS epidemic struck, that country virtually alone in Africa was doing well because its tribal structures and institutions had remained responsible and responsive to the tribal members, in great part because the country was spared the worst of colonialism but also because the best of the old tribal systems of Africa had not been destroyed but had been built upon responsibly by legitimate and authentic tribal elders, the country's substantial diamond wealth going to aid the people. In South Korea, the strict and cruel old military governments had long given way, under specific planning, to elected leaders and to highly vociferous elections.

In the end, ironically, it was these countries – and these countries alone – that had actually 'done it overnight', if you consider 'overnight' to be a mere one or two generations. These countries had 'worked' always for very specific reasons and because of very deliberate measures taken by serious leaders who cared about their own ambitions, but also cared about their country's standing in the world and about their people's progress. These men and women were able to hammer out, according to their own cultural memories and proclivities, programmes that incorporated representative government, forms of economic freedom, cultural empowerment, religious and ethnic tolerance, tight security against radical forces of either end of the spectrum, good investment and a reasonable degree of incorruptability. It was surely no accident that, in all of these countries, the changes were for the most part built upon the nature of their culture and the nature of their people.

Finally, out of the despair that was by then driving so many societies, more and more were now studying the Tunisian way. Algeria was one, Egypt was another, Morocco yet another. Belatedly and out of desperation, like the Tunisians 15 years before, they too had moved to wrest control of the countryside and villages from their own bitter Islamists; they had purged the mosques and madrasahs of their radical preachers, placing them under greater state control (which actually meant freeing them from radicalism), and had imprisoned many violent Islamists. Then they had to make a start on some of the social welfare programmes and policies that Tunisia had begun years earlier. Even the hoary old Organisation of African Unity, that quintessentially helpless Third World institution of futility, officially dissolved itself, of its own accord, and became a new economic grouping that at least stated itself in modern terms.

The New Shape of Adventure
All I could think of was that, in today's schismatised and disintegrating world, the road that I saw stretched out before me, this mosaic of factors that one saw coming together across national lines, was the true and overwhelmingly important new adventure of our times, in which the names to remember were no longer Casablanca or Coventry but Muscat and Singapore, Taipei and Tunis.

The great Italian explorer Marco Polo, in circling and recircling the globe from the beginning of his explorations in 1271, discovered asphalt in Baku, undertook missions in the service of Kublai Khan and for a time languished as a prisoner of war in Genoa. At the end of his book, he added mischievously, 'And I only told half of what I saw.' The valiant Moroccan Ibn Battuta, 'Prince of Travellers' as they called him, logged 75,000 miles in the 14th century in 29 years of tireless journeying through more than 40 different countries. As he headed off towards Yemen, the source of the Arab peoples, he wrote rhapsodically that, 'I dreamed that I was on the wing of a huge bird.' The late British explorer Wilfred Thesiger crossed and recrossed the Empty Quarter of Saudi Arabia in the 1940s and '50s, and wrote eloquently of the roots, the grace and the courtesies of the peoples of the Arabian sands.

They were seeing things for the first time that their more prosaic brothers and sisters never dared imagine. They were discovering new peoples, new cultures, new mountain ranges, new products, new jungles and new deserts, with the passion of eternally searching lovers. But their discoveries were of the things in this world. They were not transforming whole peoples from within so that they could live decently in the modern world. Those discoveries were being left to this plucky little band of countries that were trying to 'do it' in a very different and uniquely effective way.

The Road to Somewhere

Habib Ben Yahia once told me, 'This is not a doctrine for sale.' Zine El Abidine Ben Ali put it a slightly different way. 'I do not think it is appropriate to speak of exporting models,' he said, 'just as it is inconceivable that we should accept ready-made solutions brought in from elsewhere. To put it simply, we say that our experience can enrich that of others, just as our experience has been enriched by the lessons we have learned from others.'

Yet there is more to it than that. The doctrine may not be for sale, but it is certainly for study, although it means living with complication and ambivalence and eschewing the fickle certainty of revolution and rebellion.

For the final truth is that Tunisia was not 'a happening' in the popular sense of the modern world. Tunisia 'happened' the way it did because intelligent, serious, determined, historically-aware men and women made it happen. At the same time, Tunisia is not blessed (or cursed, depending upon your outlook) by oil or mineral riches. It does not have a homogeneous population, a simple, linear history or a huge, rich land mass. There is an ancillary lesson here. If they could do it, then many other countries can do it too; but many just don't know how to do it. In fact, the Tunisia experience spoke a daring truth – that not all people are immediately ready for democracy; but, even more daring, that all people could be.

The question was not whether other countries had to go through a Tunisian-style process, but whether there was really any other way to do it. The indisputable fact is that, wherever development has taken place in the modern age, it has adopted certain qualities of the Tunisian way and wherever it is seriously contemplated, it will have to consider the Tunisian lessons. It is not that the Tunisian experiment is perfect but that it actually works, when so many do not.

In addition, the danger of 'not doing it' became far more real after 9/11 and the advent of massive, world-wide terrorism and its use of weapons of mass destruction. For the radical solutions, so long fashionable, actually set back progress and may stop it altogether in many societies well into the future. How will Central Africa ever emerge from the horrors of Rwanda, the Congo, Burundi; how will West Africa survive the wars in Sierra Leone, Liberia, and now the Ivory Coast? They may be turned back from civilisation for at least this lifetime. The idea that there can be an alternative to staged and evolutionary growth no longer seems possible. There is nothing neutral or even, at best, static in a world where human beings have awakened to their potential and to their equality. Instead, without rational development, there now looms as inevitable only the collapse, chaos and oppression of a Yugoslavia, an Algeria, or a Chechnya.

One of the rules of the 20th century, then, was that, if countries don't move forward in development, they inevitably and irrevocably move backwards. The world can no longer afford to support countries that are not developing – the peace, and very likely the sanity, of the world depends upon it.

What an 'Ordinary' Country

When I walked around downtown Tunis on my last trip, I began to have the strange feeling that this was an 'ordinary' country. I turned the phrase over in my mind, tried it out on my tongue and then more or less rejected it, because Tunisia wasn't really ordinary at all (even though I had meant it as a compliment). Few people, as ordinary as most of them are, and few countries, as far from exceptional as they are, actually want to be thought of as ordinary. So instead, I began to use the more amenable word 'normal', despite its being intrinsically boring to many people.

For while the rest of the Middle East, and indeed much of the world, was collapsing and disintegrating, a simple, daily-bread normality was, for the most part, to be found in Tunisia. People were going to work, stopping to chat on the streets, busy because there was so much to do. Nine thousand NGOs offered every kind of diversion, not to speak of the beautiful beaches, the restaurants and the challenge of 'Europe' right out there on the horizon. They didn't need any revolutions, nor even any rebellions; and unless every indicator was wrong, Tunisians were still willing to give their leaders a long political leash as they continued to make their way through the minefields of development and change.

In other Arab countries, rabidly disaffected and religiously distraught youths were attacking tourists as the symbol of the outsider, of the foreigner, of the eternal colonialist forever lurking. In Tunisia, polls showed that 94 percent found the country's massive influx of foreigners fully compatible with Tunisian interests and customs.

In other Arab countries, the 'woman problem' was a genuine problem. In Tunisia, not only were women working and excelling in every conceivable field, but studies showed an increasingly egalitarian male-female marriage relationship, in which couples were essentially concerned with their children and their marital relationships and taken up very little with social and political problems, because those areas were so well taken care of already.

'You see,' my old friend Habib Ben Yahia said to me that last day as we sat in his new office, 'we didn't inherit in our civilisation the idea of "the winner respecting the loser" and "the loser not trying to kill the winner." Yet today we are pragmatic and rational, and we are trying to reflect and find solutions. We are not doctrinaire. When we see failure or difficulties that cannot be solved, we think harder.' He paused, and sighed; it was a tired sigh but it was also a sigh of determination. 'The United States had two centuries of common history,' he went on, thoughtfully. 'We do not. Please give us a chance. We are not finished.'

When I left his office that day, I told him for the record that I was going back to the hotel to work. In fact, I secretly doubled back to Sidi Bou Said, where I sat for several delicious hours at the Café des Nattes, as happy as the black and white cats that were leaping from rooftop to café and from café to exquisite doorway in the magical city.

It had been a beautiful day and Tunisians, some in modern dress and many still in traditional costume, mixed easily with tourists from all over Europe, admiring all the lovely things in the shops and lingering over coffee and drinks in the picturesque little restaurants and bars. I looked, but I did not see any revolutionaries marching down the streets promising the perfect society, nor any utopian dreamers who would either be crushed by the tanks of the righteous when the revolution came or be destroyed by their own grandiosity. I saw no-one who looked even a bit afraid and no-one who looked remotely persecuted. I sighted not a single suicide-bomber anywhere, since the Tunisians had found other ways of self-assertion, of saying, 'We exist' or, even better, 'We exist with you.'

I thought about our road in the Sahara, but I did not need to wonder how Tarzan was doing out on that desert expanse with the white stripe stretching so boldly and bravely down the centre. Only recently, I had heard to my immense amusement that Tarzan had been on Tunisian television proudly displaying the column I had written about him and soberly explaining to the viewers how this clearly illustrated that he was being recognised around the world. I had sent him a copy of the piece, on what seemed to me to be the merest chance that he might actually get it at the obscure desert address he had given me – and he did. At the same time, *Newsweek International* had featured a long piece on Tunisia entitled 'Tunisia, The Country That Works'. I accepted the blow to my putative 'copyright' – when one has a brilliant insight, one has to expect poachers.

And I thought about our road, the very road to somewhere with the white line down the centre. What had they built there now? What had they connected this week? Even as I wondered, I felt all around me the benign, beautiful and transforming hand of the holy Sufi marabout and saint who had founded Sidi Bou and whose tomb was only two flights of steep stairs up from the café, reaching out over us like a blessing. He had died, they had told me, during sunset prayers.

Together, the Tunisians, the tourists, the cats and I watched the day end and quietly observed the vivid orange, pink and purple sun slipping down into the brilliant blue Mediterranean.

I was filled with a simple joy as I suddenly realised how wonderful it was to be in such a very 'ordinary' and 'normal' country.

A BRIEF OUTLINE of TUNISIAN HISTORY

814 BC   Traditional date for the foundation of Carthage by Phoenician settlers led by the legendary Queen Dido.

6th century BC   Jews escaping the destruction of the First Temple in Jerusalem by the Babylonians come to Djerba Island in the South and establish a new temple there.

264 to 146 BC   The three Punic Wars between Carthage and Rome, including Hannibal's famous expedition with thousands of ethnically heterogeneous troops and elephants crossing the Alps between 218 and 202 BC and ending with the defeat of Carthage.

146 BC to 439 AD   The establishment of the first Roman Colony in Africa or 'Ifriqiya' and its attachment to the Roman Empire. Carthage was rebuilt during this time, in 45 BC.

439 AD   Takeover of Carthage briefly by the Vandals.

533 AD   Takeover of Carthage by the Byzantines.

647-698 AD   The Arab Islamic period begins as Muslim warriors pour across North Africa, carrying the banners of the new religion of Islam with them. The brilliant city of Kairouan is founded in 670 and the Arabs take Carthage in 698, the same year as the death of the famous Berber resistance leader, Kahina, and of the Berber resistance against the Arabs. In 689, the great Sufi marabout-sage, Sidi Bou Said Al Beji, who founded Sidi Bou Said, dies in his white and blue cliffside town, becoming an historic symbol of the kind and loving side of Islam.

711 AD   Muslim armies pour across the Straits of Gibraltar to Spain and form the great Moorish empire of al Andalus, which will last for 800 years.

800-909 AD   Islam expands, the famous Zeitouna Mosque is constructed in Tunis and the Aghlabid Dynasty begins.

909-1159   The Fatimid and Zirides dynasties take power.

1148-1159   The Normans come to Tunisia, and occupy the land until 1159 when they are expelled and when Tunis becomes the capital of the province of Ifriqiya.

1159-1230   The Almohad dynasty unites the Maghreb countries with Muslim Andalusia or al Andalus.

1228-1249   Consolidation of Hafsid control over Tunisia, as the Hafsids break away from the Almohads and establish another new dynasty, now based in Tunis.

1270   The doomed crusade of King Louis IX in Tunisia begins, but before the French monarch dies in Tunisia, he falls in love with Sidi Bou Said.

1300s Ibn Khaldun writes from Tunis, propounding his 'science of culture' from the now-famous Zeitouna Mosque. He will become known as the 'first sociologist'.

1492 The Muslim Moors are expelled from the Spain they ruled so brilliantly for nearly 800 years, together with the Jews, and the Inquisition takes power. Between 1492 and 1611, probably as many as 100,000 Moors will flee to Tunisia, lending it a strong Moorish flavour.

1574 Tunisia becomes part of the Ottoman Empire, leading to the Husseinite Dynasty. The Ottomans evict the Hapsburgs, who have also had their day in Tunisia. The Hafsid Dynasty collapses, and Tunisia becomes a province of the Ottoman Empire. The Turkish deys and beys now rule Tunisia.

1837-1855 Reign of Ahmed Bey and the first attempts at political and social reforms based upon the Turkish reformist spirit. The Fundamental Law is passed in 1857, giving rights and opportunities to all subjects of the Regency, something unheard of in the Middle East at this time.

1861 Tunisia's first Constitution is promulgated and the government contracts its first international loan in 1863, while at the same time, increased taxation triggers rural revolts.

1873-1877 The years of the brilliant reform ministry of Khereddin al-Tunisi, brought to Tunisia as an Egyptian mameluke fighter. He became Prime Minister and one of Tunisian history's most brilliant figures.

1881-1956 The French occupy Tunisia and the French Protectorate is established on May 12, 1881. French occupation is sealed in the Treaty of Bardo, followed by the La Marsa Convention which establishes the Protectorate officially. This leads to the anti-colonial resistance, led mostly by the Neo-Destour Party of independence fighter Habib Bourguiba, which persists for nearly 75 years.

1920 The resistance begins publication of *La Tunisie Martyre*; the Destour Party is organised; the General Confederation of Tunisian Workers is formed; Habib Bourguiba forms the more representative Neo-Destour Party out of the more aristocratic Destour Party; and violent anti-French demonstrations continue throughout the 1930s.

1942 German troops occupy Tunisia, while US and British forces invade from Algeria. Tunis is liberated by the Allies in 1943 and Bourguiba returns from exile to continue his work for the Allies and for the independence of Tunisia.

1956 Tunisian independence is granted by France on March 20, 1956, andthe innovative Personal Status Code, another immense step forward in the Arab world, is passed on August 13.

1957 On July 25 the last bey, Amin Bey, is deposed and Habib Bourguibabecomes the first president of the newly-proclaimed Republic of Tunisia. Women voted for the first time in the municipal elections of May 5, shocking the rest of the Arab world.

1958 All French troops are withdrawn from Tunisia except for the Bizerte naval base and the Sahara. Their presence there allows Bourguiba to divide his budget between education and social programmes and largely to ignore security concerns. The dinar is introduced as the national currency.

1959 Independent Tunisia's first Constitution of the Republic is adopted on June 1.

1960 On February 18, President Bourguiba publicly discourages the Ramadan fast so the country can move faster economically. On November 13, 250,000 acres of French-owned farm land is seized by the government in the first step of the agricultural reform. Various crises ensue over the Yugoslav-style state-planning, and French and Tunisian forces clash in Bizerte. The French finally evacuate the base on October 15, 1963, and all remaining foreign-owned farm land is nationalised in 1964 to make way for more productive modern management.

1969 The National Assembly signs a partial association agreement with the European Economic Community and new investment laws are passed. Tunisia's journey towards economic liberalisation has begun.

1974 On January 12, plans are announced for a merger between Libya and Tunisia, but they are stillborn. On September 14, the National Assembly names Bourguiba President-for- Life.

1979 The Arab League, which in earlier years had so spurned Bourguiba and his ideas, meets for the first time in Tunis and soon takes up residence there.

1981 The first sentences are imposed on scores of radical Islamists in the Movement of the Islamic Tendency. Militants soon respond with student riots at the University of Tunis and the threat of the first radical Islamic takeover of an Arab country in the Middle East becomes real.

1982 The Palestine Liberation Organisation transfers its headquarters to Tunis, leading to the Israeli air raids on their compounds in Tunis in 1985.

1986-1988 President Bourguiba's actions become increasingly erratic. He divorces his wife and accuses his son of conspiracy and arrests Rached Ghannouchi, leader of the Islamics. Meanwhile, a young intelligence officer named Zine El Abidine Ben Ali is making his way up the chain of command, being named Minister of the Interior and Prime Minister.

1987 Prime Minister Ben Ali succeeds President Bourguiba on 7 November as President of the country after Bourguiba's physicians proclaim him unable to continue assuming the duties of the office. The new President is sworn in by Parliament. He is formally elected President on April 1, l989. In the 1994 elections, the accession of the opposition to Parliament occurs for the first time in the history of independent Tunisia.

1987   The first 'National Pact' to liberalise the political process is signed between President Bourguiba, national organisations and opposition leaders.

1995   Tunisia becomes the first North African and Arab country to sign a marketing agreement with the European Community, thus beginning a long and arduous, but potentially enriching, process by which the country will effectively – economically – become part of Europe by 2007.

1999   In elections on October 24, President Ben Ali is re-elected by an overwhelming majority for a third term. His Democratic Constitutional Rally party, the successor to the Neo-Destour Party, keeps its majority in the Chamber of Deputies but the opposition garners 20 percent of the 182 seats, while the number of women in Parliament increases to 21.

1999-2001   Various steps are taken in the areas of electoral reform to open the way for multi-party elections and for incorporating human rights into the constitution, thus providing Tunisians with additional constitutional protections. The country's leadership hails these steps as the next rung on the development ladder.

SUGGESTED READING

Ajami, Fouad, *The Arab Predicament*, Cambridge University Press, Cambridge, 1981

Anthony, John, *Tunisia: a Personal View of a Timeless Land*, Charles Scribner's Sons, New York, 1961

Borowiec, Andrew, *Modern Tunisia: A Democratic Apprenticeship*, Praeger Publishers, Westport, CT., 1998

Brown, L. Carl, 'Bourguiba and Bourguibism Revisited: Reflections and Interpretation', *The Middle East Journal*, The Middle East Institute, Washington D.C., Volume 55, No. 1, Winter, 2001

Chaabane, Sadok, *Ben Ali on The Road to Pluralism in Tunisia*, American Educational Trust, Washington D.C., 1997

Cooley, John K., *Baal, Christ and Mohammed: Religion and Revolution in North Africa*, Holt, Rinehart and Winston, New York, 1965

Dillman, Bradford, 'Facing the Market in North Africa', *The Middle East Journal*, The Middle East Institute, Volume 55, No. 2, Washington D.C. Spring, 2001

Dunn, Michael C., *Renaissance or Radicalism? Political Islam: The Case of Tunisia's al-Nahda*, International Estimate, Washington D.C., 1992

Edwards, Mike, 'Tunisia: Sea, Sand, Success', *National Geographic*, Washington D.C., Vol. 157, No. 2, February, 1980

Hermassi, Abdelbaki, *The Islamist Dilemma*, Ithaca Press, London 1992

Ibn Khaldun, *The Muqaddimah*, Princeton University Press, Princeton, 1966

Jeune Afrique, 'How the Islamists Have Been Defeated', No. 2000-2001 of 11-24 May, 1999, Paris

Kaplan, Robert D., 'Le Kef, Tunisia: Roman Africa', *The Atlantic Monthly*, Boston, June 2001

Khadduri, Majid, *Arab Contemporaries: The Role of Personalities in Politics*, Johns Hopkins University Press, Baltimore, London, 1975

Klotchkoff, Jean-Claude, *Tunisia Today*, Les Editions du Jaguar, Paris

Lewis, Bernard, 'What Went Wrong?' *The Atlantic Monthly*, Boston, January, 2002

Ling, Dwight L., *Tunis: From Protectorate to Republic*, Indiana University Press, Indiana, 1967

Marks, Jon, & Ford, Mark, *Tunisia: Stability and Growth in the New Millennium*, Euromoney Books, London, 2001

Nickerson, Jane Soames, *A Short History of North Africa: From Pre-Roman Times to the Present*, The Devin-Adair Company, New York 1961

Perkins, Kenneth J., *Historical Dictionary of Tunisia*, The Scarecrow Press, Inc., Metuchen, N.J., & London, 1989

Rossi, Pierre, *Bourguiba's Tunisia*, Editions Kahia, Tunis, 1967

Rudebeck, Lars, *Party and People: A Study of Political Change in Tunisia*, Frederick A. Praeger, Inc., Publishers, New York, 1969

Saint Augustine, *Confessions*, Thomas Nelson, Inc., Nashville, Tennessee, 1999

Salem, Norma, *Habib Bourguiba, Islam and the Creation of Tunisia*, Croom Helm, London, 1984

Spencer, William, *The Land and People of Tunisia*, J. B. Lippincott Company, Philadelphia and New York, 1967

Stiglitz, Joseph E., *Globalization and its Discontents*, W.W. Norton & Company, Inc., New York, 2003

Tomkinson, Michael, *Michael Tomkinson's Tunisia*, Michael Tomkinson Publishing, Hammamet, Tunisia, 1985

United Nations Development Programme, Arab Fund for Economic and Social Development, *Arab Human Development Report 2002*, The United Nations, New York, 2002; and *Human Development Report 2002: Deepening Democracy in a Fragmented World*, The United Nations, New York, 2002

Wright, Robin, *Sacred Rage: The Wrath of Militant Islam*, Simon and Schuster, New York, 1989

Zakaria, Fareed, 'The Rise of Illiberal Democracy', *Foreign Affairs*, The Council on Foreign Relations, New York, November/December, 1997

Zartman, I. William, *Man, State and Society in Contemporary Maghreb*, Praeger Publishers, New York, 1973

— *Tunisia: The Political Economics of Reform*, Lynne Rieser, Boulder, 1991

Zine El Abidine Ben Ali, Speech by the President on the 15th Anniversary of The Change, and Speech by the President on the occasion of the National Day of Culture, May 27, 1999, Carthage Palace, Carthage

INDEX